LATIMER STUDY 83

YOUR WILL BE DONE

*Exploring Eternal Subordination,
Divine Monarchy and
Divine Humility*

BY MICHAEL J. OVEY

The Latimer Trust

Published by the Latimer Trust May 2016

The Latimer Trust (formerly Latimer House, Oxford) is a conservative Evangelical research organisation within the Church of England, whose main aim is to promote the history and theology of Anglicanism as understood by those in the Reformed tradition. Interested readers are welcome to consult its website for further details of its many activities.

The Latimer Trust
London N14 4PS UK
Registered Charity: 1084337
Company Number: 4104465
Web: www.latimertrust.org
E-mail: administrator@latimertrust.org

CONTENTS

Your Will Be Done:
Exploring Eternal Subordination, Divine Monarchy and Divine Humility

'The Trinity isn't a fixed hierarchy. It's more like a company of actors that take different roles depending on the play they're performing.'[1]

---

[1] Sam Wells. 'Can we still call God Father?' a sermon preached in Duke University Chapel on June 7, 2009 http://chapel-archives.oit.duke.edu/documents/sermons/June7CanwestillcallGodFather.pdf accessed 13/11/12

1   Introduction[1]

1.1   *The immediate issue – a new Arianism?*

It has been argued that those of us who hold that the Son is eternally subordinate to the Father have fallen into the old heresy of Arianism. The charge involves three major elements:

- **Historical:** Eternal subordination is a recent invention (often perceived as a last-ditch position for those opposed to the ordination of women to the presbyterate or their consecration to the episcopate);

- **Biblical:** Eternal subordination is unfounded in Scripture and indeed contrary to it; and

- **Theological:** Eternal subordination has catastrophic effects in terms of the exercise of power.

The charge is, of course, serious, since Arianism was subjected to anathema at the Council of Nicaea in 325. To accuse someone of Arianism is to imply they are simply not Christian.

As such, those who make this accusation are not only logically committed to barring from ordination to the presbyterate those of us holding to eternal subordination but are also committed to refusing to accept as fellow-believers those of us holding that view, for, of course, Arians are to be seen as heretics. Conversely, if the accusation is false and it is not true that those holding to eternal subordination are necessarily Arian, then clearly those who have made the false accusation need to repent of what is at least the sin of schism.

Those who have made the charge, therefore, are playing – to put it mildly – for high stakes.

1.2   *Summary of the answer to the charge*

Since the charge has been made on historical, biblical and theological levels, it must be examined and answered on all three levels: historical;

---

[1]   This monograph is based on a paper submitted to evangelical bishops of the Church of England in early January 2015.

biblical and theological. This involves some quite technical argument and I must ask the reader for perseverance: too much is at stake to give these matters short shrift. As we do this, we will find that the relevant biblical and historical material addresses the issue of the relation between the Father and the Son from a particular perspective. That perspective is how the Father and the Son can both be fully divine without undermining two ideas that are closely related to each other, namely, monotheism and the divine monarchy. Put sharply, we must look at the traditional but obvious question of why Father and Son are not two gods, and in particular how the Bible addresses that issue.

We will argue that the history of the Nicene/Arian controversy, the biblical material and the resultant theology alike focus on the fundamental proposition that the Son is a true Son. Since the Son is a true son, two things follow: first, he shares his Father's nature, and is therefore fully God; and secondly he is in an eternal relationship as son in which he submits to his Father, as sons do, something aptly described as subordination. Further, the Son and Father love each other but they love each other in ways that belong to their individual standings as Son and Father. The Son loves his Father in a characteristically filial way and the Father loves his Son in a characteristically paternal way. So the Father loves paternally, instructing and providing inheritance for his Son; the Son loves filially, obeying and doing his Father's will; and in this way each glorifies the other. It is in this way that the true sonship of the Son preserves the monotheistic oneness of God and in particular his sole rule or monarchy. This eternal subordination of the Son preserves the divine monarchy. Eternal subordination is integral to answering the charge that the Father and the Son are two gods. The argument that the Son only obeys in his human nature does not provide an answer to the question posed in the Bible and by patristic theologians, namely how in eternity the Father and Son are not two Gods. Instead that argument tends to gloss over how the Son derives his claim to cosmic monarchy from the gift of his Father and what that implies for the eternal relations between the Father and his Son.

This position in which the Son is subordinate to his Father as a son has historical precedent since it is adopted by the great defenders of the Nicene faith, Athanasius of Alexandria and Hilary of Poitiers, and is echoed at points in Augustine. It is rooted in Scripture, especially John's Gospel. It is used by Athanasius and Hilary precisely in their claim that they remain monotheists rather than polytheists. Theologically this opens the prospect of asymmetrical personal relationships concerning power and love. In these relationships, power is genuinely other-personed, and is not self-seeking; further, authority, obedience and other-personed love can be seen as properly related to each other rather than as mutually exclusive or obscuring each other.

This position is not Arianism, since Arianism at its heart asserts that the Second Person of the Trinity is a creature, while this Nicene position stresses that as a true son he is not a creature, for sons are begotten not made.

This argument will be substantiated by looking at historical, biblical and theological issues. We will also briefly examine some further arguments relating to the two natures and two wills of the incarnate Son and how they may affect the argument concerning eternal subordination. We will find in particular that consideration of Jesus' prayer in Gethsemane indicates that an orthodox 'two wills' understanding of the incarnate Son does not conflict with the true Son's eternal subordination in his relation as a person with his Father.

1.3   The broader context

Before moving to these areas, it is helpful to say something more about the broad context in which this charge has been made.

1.3.1   Debates over the role of women

Part of the broader context is the debate over women in the presbyterate and episcopate, as well as marriage more generally. It is helpful to sketch out now how the eternal subordination of the Son might or might not affect debates over the role of women.

First, the Trinitarian revelation of God tells us of Father, Son and Holy Spirit. To state the obvious, a father-son relationship is not the same as a husband-wife relationship nor does a father-son relationship necessarily by itself determine the different kinds of relationship that may exist between men and women generally, whether inside or outside the church. One may exegete 1 Timothy 2:11-15 in a non-traditional way while asserting the eternal subordination or subjection of the Son.

Secondly, the language of headship, which has proved so contentious, does not explicitly arise in the context of women's ordination.[2] Rather the headship language of 1 Corinthians 11:3, which

---

[2]   We need to bear in mind in any event that while 'ordination' in its current sense certainly overlaps with the New Testament presbyterate, it does not map onto it completely.

puts in parallel the headship of God to Christ, 'man' to 'woman' and Christ to man, addresses other issues in the corporate life of God's people than the presbyterate. This remains so whether one takes the reference in that verse to 'man' and 'woman' as referring to male and female or to husband and wife. I appreciate that headship language has been strongly associated with a conservative view on 1 Timothy 2 and I would endorse what I think the language is largely trying to express, but for the sake of clarity it is worth saying that the God : Christ and the husband/man : wife/woman headship relationships do not necessarily *automatically* transfer directly across to 1 Timothy 2 and its context of church order, although they are clearly relevant.

Thirdly, while seeing the Son-Father relation as one of subordination does not necessarily determine male-female relations, it does establish that there can be an eternal and ethically pure relationship of submission or subordination between those who are ontologically equal, that is, equal at the level of being, value or nature. This has huge implications for a culture which is deeply suspicious of power relationships: it shows there can be relationships of authority and power which are not necessarily sinful simply by virtue of being relationships of power. This does have implications for the ordination of women to the presbyterate in this limited sense: one cannot say that the refusal to ordain women to the presbyterate necessarily means that women are being treated as beings who are lesser at the level of nature than men – that they are ontological inferiors.

1.3.2   Language

The language used in the current debate manages to be both highly emotive but inconsistently employed. We have used the term 'eternal subordination', but the idea this is meant to express has been variously put: as the Son's submission, subjection, or obedience to the Father in their eternal relationship. Alternative expressions use terminology such as the Father's eternal 'headship' or the Father's super-ordination.

Talk of hierarchy, subjection, subordination, submission and obedience carries strong resonances for us of exploitation and sinful inequality. Further, shifting from one term, say 'hierarchy', to another, such as 'submission', can smack simply of using more euphemistic terms for something that remains inherently wrong. In fact, when we talk of hierarchy, subjection, subordination, headship, submission or super-ordination, a key issue is whether the Son is in a relationship of eternal obedience to the Father. At their best, the different sets of language try to draw this out.

1.3.3 Current cultural suspicions

In all of this, we must bear in mind that our own western cultural attitudes towards power and obedience are both complex and deeply ambiguous. On the one hand there is considerable suspicion towards authority and power-holders,[3] as if the mere possession of authority is ethically questionable, but on the other hand this is a time in the modern west of intense 'juridification', by which we basically mean the extension of legal regulation into more and more of life.[4] To that extent, the citizen has an ambiguous experience: she or he is both inculcated in suspicion of authority while finding more and more of our daily lives regulated by it. There can be something Kafka-esque about contemporary experience of our regulated culture.

This means that the authority question is not, of course, simply restricted to male-female relations in church, or relations between husbands and wives. It is vital to grasp this. Authority is also a relevant factor in relations more generally in church between presbyterate and laity, between children and parents and between citizens and the state or ruling authorities. The Bible, naturally, addresses all of these. Further, authority and its limits are highly relevant matters for our experience as employees and employers, or as managers in an employment context and those managed.

An additional complicating factor in these relationships where authority is present is that the New Testament envisages humility and obedience as virtues of the Christian's daily life. But if we are to think that relations of authority and power are inherently bad, then a riddle arises at this point: how is one to be humbly obedient as, for instance, a citizen with respect to the state (as Romans 13:1ff indicates) if one should be denouncing a citizen's obedience to state authorities as arising from an inherently ethically bad relationship? To this extent, the question of the eternal subordination of the Son bears on what could count as a godly life for a Christian.

---

[3] The influence of F Nietzsche and M Foucault is hugely significant, but significant too is the work of J-F Lyotard who notes not only apparent incredulity towards meta-narratives but that they can operate 'terroristically'.

[4] L Blichner and A Molander identify five distinguishable but related dimensions in which this basic idea unfolds. ('What is Juridification?' Centre for European Studies (Oslo), working paper 14, 2005).

1.4 Current thinking behind the charge of Arianism

Of course, the charge that the Son's eternal subordination is necessarily Arian can be put in different ways. Two are of particular concern here.

1.4.1 No obedience at all

Thus some argue that the Son does not obey the Father at all, whether in the Incarnation or not. A very important and influential example is J Moltmann. Moltmann points to Jesus' use of the 'Abba' term.[5] For Moltmann, this indicates two things: first, 'Abba' shows intense intimacy between Father and Son. This aspect of Moltmann's argument is of course largely uncontroversial and advocates of the Son's eternal subordination would happily agree.[6] The sting comes in Moltmann's second point about 'Abba': this is to the effect that the intimacy of 'Abba' excludes authority between Father and the Son.[7] It is, of course, perfectly possible to agree with Moltmann on the intimacy point without agreeing on the second point, the exclusion of authority. We will consider later whether 'Abba' means an intimacy without authority.

We must understand, though, that this is part of a wider project for Moltmann, in which he wants to question the existence of authority in a number of human relationships: within the church, within the family and within the state.[8] The idea of addressing God as 'Abba' and therefore with an intimacy that excludes authority becomes a touchstone for Moltmann of God's 'kingdom':

> In this kingdom God is not the Lord; he is the merciful Father. In this kingdom there are no servants; there are only God's free children. In this kingdom what is required is not obedience and submission it is love and free participation.[9]

And Moltmann sees this ethos as carrying over into other relationships:

> The Abba-nearness of God evidently fills and permeates this new messianic community to such a degree that the function and

---

[5] J Jeremias is in the background here with his insistence on the distinctiveness of 'abba' terminology .

[6] And the contention does not first arise with Moltmann. He himself cites J Jeremias.

[7] See Moltmann, J, *The Trinity and the Kingdom of God: the doctrine of God* trans. Kohl, M (London: SCM, 1981): p 69 n 17; p 70 n. 19.

[8] In view of the importance of the employment relationship in the 21st century West, this too should be reviewed for its power dynamics.

[9] Moltmann, *The Trinity* p 70.

authority of the earthly father vanishes.[10]

Of course, the corollary of this is that introducing authority into our doctrine of God will contaminate our other relationships. Thus:

> In our culture, religious worship of God as "Lord and Father" has legitimated both the rule of the father in the family and "father of the land" in the state, just as it has legitimised the fatherly rule of male priests and pastors in religion.[11]

This means that for Moltmann and his followers, eternal subordination whether we call it 'Arianism' or not, is catastrophic because of its authoritarian tendencies. It is no idle 'angels-dancing-on-the-head-of-a-pin' issue of abstract theology. His point is that it *legitimates* a certain power-based way of conducting relationships amongst human beings.

In effect, Moltmann has an antithesis between power/authority on the one hand and relational or personal intimacy on the other. Each rules the other out. Most sharply, 'obedience and submission' are excluded by 'love and free participation'.[12] Equally, if 'obedience and submission' are present, then 'love and free participation' are not. This antithesis is highly significant, but scarcely unique to Moltmann: similar points have been made by Clark Pinnock and other members of the Open Theist movement.[13] More generally, misgivings are voiced about those holding to a strong account of God as Lord.[14] This antithesis between authority and relational intimacy obviously does have consequences for the relationship between the Father and the Son, but also more generally and to the relation between humans and God in particular. For this reason, Moltmann's line of argument resonates with a significant current theological and social mood.

---

[10] Moltmann J, *History and the Triune God*. Bowden, J. (Trans.) (London: SCM, 1991), pp 11,12.

[11] Moltmann, *History and the Triune God* p 2.

[12] Moltmann, *The Trinity* p 70.

[13] E.g. Pinnock, C (ed.), *The Grace of God, the Will of Man* (Grand Rapids: Zondervan, 1989) p ix 'The question can be put this way: Is God the absolute Monarch who always gets his way, or is God rather the loving Parent who is sensitive to our needs even when we disappoint him and frustrate some of his plans.'

[14] E.g. Williams, R 'Barth on the Triune God' in Sykes, S W (ed.) *Karl Barth – Studies of his Theological Methods* (Oxford: Clarendon Press. 1979), pp 189-90 '...[Y]et power, lordship, the master-slave relationship, all play an uncomfortably large part in Barth's system.'

1.4.2   Only a human obedience

Another significant argument is that the Son does obey but only in his human nature in the Incarnation. Obedience does not extend to the eternal relationship between the Father and the Son.[15]

Again, it is helpful to be precise about what is at stake here. This argument is very different in this respect from the one put by Moltmann and others. Here the issue is not whether we see obedience on the part of the Son in the Gospels. This line of argument concedes that we do, but asserts that the Son obeys **only as a human**. Those arguing for eternal subordination agree that the Son does have this human obedience. In fact, this is critical for Reformation accounts of justification by faith which stress that Jesus keeps the law of God for us in our place so that we have a human righteousness imputed to us.[16] What is at stake is whether, in addition to an obedience in his humanity, the Son is also eternally subordinate by virtue of his eternal relation as son. Put sharply, the issue is: 'what relational contours follow from the eternal sonship of the Son?'

Naturally we must also observe that some things are indeed attributable to the Son through his human nature: thus his experience of, say, physical weariness (e.g. John 4:6) is possible only by virtue of the Son taking a second, human, nature through the Incarnation. It is by virtue of that second nature that the Son experiences weariness. The question is whether this line of argument is also applicable to all the obedience of the Son.

1.4.3   Common factors

What tends to lie behind both approaches is the proposition that eternal obedience would mean that the Son was inferior as a being, which

---

[15] Particularly vociferous along these lines in recent years has been Kevin Giles (see bibliography: Giles 2002, 2006, 2009, 2012). P Adam in 'Honouring Jesus Christ', *Churchman* 2005 p 38 summarises Giles' position thus: 'Giles' basic claim is clear. It is that no 'subordination' of any kind will be found in the operations of the Triune God, except that in the Incarnation the human Jesus is subordinate to the Father.' For earlier criticism along these lines see G Bilezikian, 'Hermeneutical Bungee-Jumping: Subordination in the Godhead' *JETS* 40.1 (1997) pp 57-68. Since Giles has been so prominent, his arguments necessarily bulk large in what follows.

[16] See notably Homily 3 in the *Books of Homilies* for the declaration that Jesus is the one who keeps the law for us. His obedience is counted as our obedience. The proposition that the divine righteousness is imputed to us is associated with the 16th century theologian Osiander, who was opposed by both Lutherans and Reformed.

amounts to straight Arianism.[17] Obedience and ontological equality are incompatible.

This is not a new argument. In fact in the late phases of the Arian debate, homoian Arians argued precisely along these lines.[18] Put shortly:

a) Obedience and ontological equality are incompatible.

b) The Son clearly obeys (the homoian Arians point to instances outside the Incarnation)

c) Therefore the Son is not ontologically equal to the Father, but only a creature.

Set out like this, we see that proposition a) in this argument is in fact shared by Arians and current deniers of the eternal subordination of the Son. They differ on statements b) and c), but proposition a) is common ground. If it is true that only creatures obey, then, whether or not one thinks the Son obeys in his human nature, he certainly cannot be eternally subordinate, because if he did, then he would be a creature. To say that the Son is a creature certainly is Arian.[19]

Thus two related key questions emerge as we assess these current arguments that the Son is not eternally subordinate to the Father.

a) Is it true that only creatures obey?

b) What relational contours follow from the Son being a son?

---

[17] Notably Giles and the former Archbishop of Perth, Peter Carnley [e.g. Peter Carnley, *Reflections in Glass* (Sydney: Harper Collins, 2004)]. Even if, as Peter Adam feels ['Honouring Jesus Christ', *Churchman* 2005, pp 35-50], Carnley's charge is playing ecclesiastical politics, such an important charge must still be considered and answered.

[18] Arianism goes through several phases after its initial articulation by Arius in the early 320s. Homoian Arianism is an expression of Arianism from the late 4th century, drawing heavily on creeds such as the Sirmium *Blasphemia* of 357, with its seemingly pious stress that the Son and Father are 'like [homoios – hence homoian] as the Scriptures teach'. The Sirmium *Blasphemia* is dealt with below. Notably Augustine in the early 5th century faced homoian Arianism which used this argument: see *Arian Sermon* 34 and *Debate with Maximinus* 15.14, 18 and 23. Giles [*The Trinity and Subordinationism: the Doctrine of God and the Contemporary Gender Debate* (Downers Grove: Illinois, 2002)] does not refer to these late texts from Augustine on the Arian issue, preferring to cite from *De Trinitate*.

[19] This is explained more fully below.

1.5   Other arguments – the impact of the Dyothelite controversy

However, a further range of argument also needs to be considered. The arguments outlined above are the ones normally used to make good the charge of Arianism. Nevertheless, the eternal subordination also needs to be seen in the light of another, less frequently discussed, issue: that of the wills of the Son. This arises in the following way.

As is well known, the Council of Chalcedon 451 held that the eternal Person the Son was in two natures, divine and human. The intention of that Council was to use the framework set out in the Council of Nicaea. That framework in effect distinguished between the threeness of the Godhead in its divine Persons and their oneness in the one nature.[20] The distinction between the categories of 'Person' and 'nature' became fundamental. It means we can talk about God being both one and three without self-contradiction.

The Council of Chalcedon used that distinction in talking of one Person in two natures. That basic Chalcedonian description of one Person with two natures was applied in later councils to the question of whether the Son had one will or two, and one 'energy' (or 'way of working') or two. The Son was declared to have two wills (dyothelitism) and two energies, because he has two natures in their completeness. Since a nature would not be complete without its distinctive 'will' and energy, each nature that the Son has must have its own distinctive will and energy in this technical sense.

Yet an argument could then go like this: it is a category mistake to talk of the Son's eternal subordination or obedience, since he and his Father have only one divine will which they share. This issue too needs more extended discussion, and in particular means a close consideration of Jesus' prayer in Gethsemane.[21]

With all this in mind, we turn to the historical issues. The reason why we consider the historical issues first is that it has been argued that the eternal subordination of the Son lacks any historical precedent and is only a modern invention. As such we look first at the question whether that is

---

[20]   The opening of the Chalcedonian definition stresses its continuity with the Fathers of Nicaea. For a full discussion of the use of the Niceno-Constantinopolitan Person/Substance distinction by Chalcedon, see D Bathrellos, *The Byzantine Christ: Person, Nature, and Will in the Christology of Maximus the Confessor* (Oxford: OUP, 2004).

[21]   This was rightly seen as highly significant in the dyothelite controversy.

true, before moving to the decisive question of whether those in history who do see the eternal subordination of the Son were right to do so.

2 The Historical question

2.1 Preliminary

A key period is the prolonged debate from the Council of Nicaea (325) to
the Council of Constantinople (381). The essentials of Arianism were
teased out during this time and the debate decisively settled. The Nicene
theologians had the Arian issue staring them in the face for several
decades. It is therefore reasonable to envisage that if they thought eternal
subordination was necessarily Arian, then it very probably is. Conversely,
if they address the issue and think eternal subordination is not
necessarily Arian, then we might need to re-examine any assumption that
obedience necessarily means the Son must be a creature.

2.2 Summary of Nicene findings

In short, we will find that rather than condemning eternal
subordination as necessarily Arian, key Nicene theologians uphold it,
and do so on the basis that this is part of the Son's true sonship. They
think that eternal subordination does not mean that the Son must
necessarily be a creature. Instead, eternal subordination is part of the
rationale which upholds the key twin values of monotheism and the
divine monarchy, by showing that there is one monarchy. In this they
are in fundamental continuity with earlier Trinitarian thinking.

2.3 Background

Of course, the Arian question does not emerge from nothing. There is a
context for it, both culturally and in church history terms.

2.3.1 Cultural

Naturally, father-son relationships are not the same in all cultures. To
understand whether a position is 'Nicene' and/or 'biblical' it is worth
remembering the cultural backgrounds of both situations.

In brief, we find both in historical and biblical material that the
parent-child relation is important both for conferring status as citizen or
covenant member but also for laying down an obligation to obey on the
part of the child. In the modern cultural West we are perfectly familiar
with the first of these aspects, but have become less so with the second.

Thus, with regard to the Greco-Roman world, the reverence of sons for their fathers is well-established. The paragon of Roman virtue, Aeneas, as depicted in Vergil's Aeneid, is one who shows *pietas* to his father.[1] The tragedy of Orestes is that his duty to defend his father's honour and avenge him means that he must kill even his mother. In Roman law, of course, the paterfamilias has traditionally full disposal (*potestas*) over his own children.[2] The children get their citizenship from their father, but at the same time are also in his power (*potestas*) by virtue of his paternity. In this way sons have both civic equality with their fathers (both are citizens), but by virtue of the same relationship are under their fathers' power.

With regard to biblical material, in the Old Testament, parentage is decisive. Membership of the Abrahamic covenant is conferred by descent and to that extent one's membership of the people of Abraham is derived from one's parents and shared with them (Genesis 17:9ff).[3] However, there is also the command to honour one's parents (Exodus 20:12), which is developed in terms of obligation of obedience from sons towards parents (Deuteronomy 21:18-21). There are, then, some rough parallels with Roman law in that the father-son relationship confers both status (citizenship or membership of the covenant) and also the filial obligation to obey.

In the New Testament, Jesus comments very negatively on those who try to evade the honour obligations of the Fifth Commandment, which he clearly regards as applicable to adult sons, not just juveniles (Mark 7:9-13).[4] Paul explicitly reiterates the duty of children's obedience

---

[1]   Notably in the flight from Troy: *Aeneid* II.

[2]   *Institutes* of Gaius: 'Thus Roman citizens have their children in their *potestas* [power] if they take to wife Roman women, or even Latin or peregrine women with whom they have *conubium* (power to contract civil marriage). For, as the effect of *conubium* is that the children take the same status as their father, the result is that the children are not only Roman citizens, but are also in their father's *potestas*.' Bk 1.56. (*De Personis)* [=56. *Itaque liberos suos in potestate habent ciues Romani, si ciues Romanas uxores duxerint, uel etiam Latinas peregrinasue cum quibus conubium habeant. Cum [[sic]] enim conubium id efficiat, ut liberi patris condicionem sequantur, euenit ut non (solum) ciues Romani fiant, sed etiam in potestate patris sint.*] In this respect the *Institutes of Justinian* are substantially the same. See *Institutes of Justinian* I. ix and ix.3.

[3]   There are exceptional instances of foreigners joining the people of God, e.g. Rahab and Ruth. But clearly the immediate primary 'qualification' for circumcision as a sign of covenant membership is physical descent.

[4]   In the 'corban' dispute he is addressing an adult audience who have made oaths about the disposition of their property.

towards their parents in Ephesians 6:1 (where it is connected with the Fifth Commandment) and Colossians 3:18. These New Testament references are significant. They show that we cannot see the obedience obligations of sons as purely arising under an OT dispensation which has been fulfilled in Christ in the same way that, for instance, dietary restrictions are. The obedience obligations are not thought of as inappropriate or immoral in the renewed people of God. Rather the reverse.

These considerations are worth spelling out to prevent us assuming that the modern cultural West's pattern, where a son's ongoing obedience is culturally unfamiliar, holds completely true when looking at material in the Bible and in the Nicene period of the fourth century. In fact, the preponderance of the material in both Greco-Roman culture and in the biblical material makes one ask whether the burden of proof does not lie on those denying the subordination of the Son. Subordination to fathers is just what sons characteristically should do in these cultural settings.

2.3.2   Church history overview

For our purposes, we can envisage the relevant history in three periods:

- Pre-Nicene (pre-325)
- Nicene (325-381)
- Post-Constantinopolitan (381 and after)

This division is necessary because we have to assess whether the Nicene settlement marked a repudiation of earlier positions or a refinement in the light of a new and unfortunate development. We also have to recall that the Arian question continued to have practical traction after 381 because of the use by the later Roman Empire of Germanic mercenaries who had themselves been 'evangelised' by Arian missionaries.[5] Their presence obviously kept the issues alive as a matter of public debate in, for example, Augustine's North Africa, notwithstanding any 'official' position declared at Constantinople in 381. This in turn means that Augustine's later thoughts from about 415 onwards on this are those of

---

[5]   Probably Arian missionaries taking their cue from the position of the Sirmium *Blasphemia* – homoian Arians.

a theologian wanting to stand in line with Nicene theology but meeting some of the later developments in pro-Arian argument.[6]

2.4   *Correctly framing the historical question*

As we approach the historical issue we need to remember that our contemporary questions are not necessarily those of the patristic theologians. Obviously the discussions of the patristic period are not conducted with an eye on their implications for the ordination of women to the presbyterate or episcopate. Nor do patristic theologians necessarily have the same hermeneutics of suspicion towards the exercise of power and authority that our culture frequently shows.[7] This means some care is required when seeking perspectives on questions which were not framed for them in quite the way, perhaps, that they are now.

As we examine the relevant periods we find that a key concern centres on the issue of monotheism/divine cosmic monarchy: for the patristic theologians the two ideas are closely entwined. They are concerned to uphold the ideas both that God is one and that there is one rule (*archē*) in the cosmos. The two ideas are connected and indeed interdependent: if there is more than one rule (*archē*), then there is more than one God.[8] But if there is more than one God, then, so the argument continues, there is nothing that is 'really' God.[9] Without the divine monarchy there must necessarily be polytheism and/or atheism.[10] But if we say there is more than one God, then clearly there cannot be just one rule (*archē*). To this extent, there cannot be 'one God' if there is not 'one rule'. Divine monarchy follows from monotheism

---

[6]   Augustine clearly aligns himself with Nicene theology in *De Trinitate* I.7. He should not readily be taken as undermining it.

[7]   This does not mean the patristic theologians were blind to the misuse of power. Athanasius and Hilary certainly do criticise what they see as tyranny on the part of the emperor Constantius. They do not, however, see his position as inherently abusive.

[8]   Athanasius' comments in *Contra Gentes* 6 are representative at this point.

[9]   J Moignt catches this well in the case of the major figure of Tertullian: 'The unicity of God is, then, deduced from the existence of a single sovereignty [*seigneurie*], which can belong to only one person: *unicus Dominus*'. Moignt 'Le Probleme du Dieu Unique chez Tertullien', *RSR* 44 (1970) p 342.

[10]   For key patristic thinkers, polytheism degenerated into atheism, not least because where there were, hypothetically, many rulers, the end result was for there to be no rule, and therefore, no real god (atheism). Gregory of Nazianzen provides a classic statement of this in his *Third Theological Oration on the Son* II.

and monotheism follows from divine monarchy. Likewise, a denial of either will entail a denial of the other, so runs the patristic logic.

As we articulate this patristic concern, it is immediately apparent that patristic theology stands in no little tension with Moltmann's position, which is essentially to eliminate any kind of rule (*archē*).[11] With regard to the idea that the Son's obedience is restricted to his human nature and is not part of the eternal relationship, the question is whether this adequately safeguards the divine monarchy, and hence, whether it adequately safeguards monotheism.

As it happens, both of the major heresies we shall look at, modalism and Arianism are attempts to defend monotheism.[12] They are erroneous ways of asserting God is one.[13] But two things need to be remembered. First, the patristic theologians who refuted modalism and Arianism emphatically did not dismiss monotheism – they upheld it. Monotheism/divine monarchy was a **shared** concern for heretics (whether Arian or modalist) and orthodox alike. Secondly, this monotheistic concern is perhaps not perceived today as such a dominating issue in debates over the Son's eternal subordination.[14] At its best, the heart-beat of those denying the Son's eternal subordination can be a laudable stress on the Son's full deity. The patristic theologians would support this stress but add that the Son's full deity cannot be at the expense of monotheism/divine monarchy, and that the monotheism/divine monarchy issue must be answered. Monotheism and divine monarchy is as fundamental as the full deity of the Son.

---

[11] The incompatibility of Moltmann's views with the patristic principles is dealt with more fully below.

[12] Current academic *chic* is to see the later heresies of the 4th century as 'homoian' rather than Arian. Contemporaries in favour of the Nicene Creed did not, since they thought there were common values in the rejection by 'homoians' of the Nicene term *homoousios* (same substance) and the retention of the idea that at some level the Son was a creature (See Augustine *On Heresies*). The ancient usage is thus wider. Since the charges of Giles and others do not tend to use the modern distinctions, recourse is had here to the wider usage, since that is the range of criticism with which we are concerned.

[13] Thus Tertullian comments in *Against Praxeas* 1 that Satan has made a heresy out of the very unity of God, something that in Tertullian's context was so often the mark of orthodoxy against polytheism.

[14] Clearly, though, monotheism, and what counts as **biblical** monotheism is of concern in debates with Judaism and Islam.

3   The Pre-Nicene Period: Tertullian and the Modalist question

3.1   Modalism and the question of Monotheism and Monarchy

Arianism was not the first major 'Trinitarian heresy' the early Church endured.[1] In the third century, the issue was rather more modalism, or Monarchianism. As the name 'Monarchianism' implies,[2] the major concern of such modalists was to preserve the principle of monotheism especially as expressed in the divine cosmic monarchy. The point was that if one has two distinguishable 'Lords', then that monarchy was undermined. Hence the Father and the Son needed to be seen ultimately as one person. If they were two persons, then there were two Lords and hence two 'rules'. John 10:30 was taken by the Monarchians as decisively supportive of this idea that the Father and Son are one person.[3] To that extent, one can say that 'Father' and 'Son' are different 'roles' that the one divine person plays on the stage of history. This is frequently put in the terms of 'Father' and 'Son' being modes or ways in which God is revealed or presented to us, but not how he actually is outside history. From 'modes', of course, comes the term 'modalism' which is the general way of speaking about theologies that eliminate the genuine differences between the Persons of the Trinity. Strictly, 'Monarchianism' is one species of this more general complaint of modalism.

A leading and articulate opponent of this Monarchian version of modalism was Tertullian.[4] Tertullian was a highly influential writer in early Latin Christianity.[5] His major work on the subject is addressed

---

[1]   Although arguably, one can see Marcionism as having a Trinitarian dimension to its heresy by separating the God of creation from the God of salvation. To this extent one can see it in part as being an over-separation of the Persons related to the particular 'work' a divine Person does.

[2]   Taken from the Greek term *monarchia*.

[3]   Those arguing against Monarchianism had to find a better way of explaining John 10:30. They focused on the point that the Monarchians treated the verse as though it said 'one person', which would require the masculine form of the noun, when John actually employs the neuter, 'one thing', which fits the idea of 'one person' badly.

[4]   Fl. 200 A.D.

[5]   Some have argued that later in life Tertullian shifted to the sect of Montanism. This does not necessarily affect the validity of his argument in *Against Praxeas,* much of which has parallels in other Christian writers critiquing Monarchianism.

against one 'Praxeas'.[6] He points out that Praxeas' view '...thinks it impossible to believe in one God [*unicum deum*] unless it says that both Father, Son and Holy Spirit are one and the same [*ipsum eundemque*].'[7] For Praxeas, God's unity or unicity is at issue,[8] and this is connected to Praxeas' goal of upholding the divine monarchy. In effect the Monarchian case is intimately tied to divine cosmic monarchy. Thus, on the Monarchian argument, if one undermines the divine monarchy, then in consequence one has also undermined monotheism. Conversely if one's Trinitarian theology ensures the divine monarchy is intact, then monotheism is upheld. But, to the Monarchians, the divine monarchy was not intact if one had two 'lords'. Accordingly, the only way to allow both Father and Son to be addressed as 'lord' and 'God' was if they were in fact the same person.

This means that Tertullian's argument against Monarchian modalism has to focus on the divine cosmic monarchy and it has to show how the divine monarchy can still exist without saying Father and Son are the same person.

3.2   Summary of the rejection of Modalism

In effect we shall find that Tertullian argues that the Son is revealed to us *as truly a son* and as such his Father delegates or gives to him a full share in the divine monarchy.[9] As such, it is right to see the Son as fully God and as a distinguishable Person from his Father. Since the Son derives his rule from his Father, the divine monarchy is not subverted by being divided and the Son is subordinate to his Father outside the incarnation, that is, not just in his human nature.

3.3   Tertullian's defence of Divine Monarchy

Before we examine Tertullian any further, it is worth asking whether Tertullian is worth bothering with. Thus Giles, in his argument against eternal subordination, concedes that Tertullian introduced some

---

6   'Praxeas' may be a nickname, roughly equivalent to 'twister'.
7   *Against Praxeas* 2. Chapter references are to the Ante-Nicene Fathers edition, since this is the most readily available translation.
8   Compare the similar points made in Hippolytus' anti-Monarchian piece *Against Noetus* 2.1-3.
9   Tertullian's argument has substantial similarities to other anti-Monarchians on the divine monarchy point.

important terminology,[10] but then goes on to say that Tertullian sees the Son and Spirit 'as creations of the Father.'[11] This oversimplifies so much as to be seriously incorrect: Tertullian exegetes John 1:1 to the effect that the Word (*Logos*) is **always** with and within God, but distinguishable from him. The Word is then eternal, as Tertullian scholar E. Osborn rightly notes: 'God always had *Logos* as Reason...'[12] Tertullian's account of the Second Person as Son does have significant limitations as we shall see, but as Word/*Logos* Tertullian clearly sees the Second Person as eternal.[13] If the Word is eternal, then it has no beginning and all creatures have beginnings. To be a creature, one has to have a beginning. The Word is therefore not a creature, since it has no beginning. Hence, contrary to Giles, we cannot dismiss Tertullian simply as articulating an early form of Arianism which sees the Son as a creature.

That said, Tertullian certainly does focus on the divine cosmic monarchy. However, we need to note that this is not a mere debating point for him, a tactical concession within the Monarchian controversy. He really is committed to it and shows this by advocating and using it in other works where the issue is not Monarchianism.[14] Tertullian proceeds through several stages in making his case:[15]

- What monarchy is;

- What undermines divine monarchy;

- How the divine monarchy is organised.

We will look briefly at each.

3.3.1 *What monarchy is*

Tertullian offers the following general definition of 'monarchy', whether divine or otherwise:

---

[10] Giles *The Trinity and Subordinationism* p 61.

[11] Giles *The Trinity and Subordinationism* p 62.

[12] Osborn *Tertullian, First Theologian of the West* (Cambridge: CUP, 1997) p 124.

[13] The argument of the anti-Monarchians was that God was never without his *Logos* (Reason) and that it was impious towards the **First** Person to say that there was a point when he was *alogos*, which has the implication of being 'without reason', that is, irrational.

[14] Notably in his works *Against Hermogenes* and *Against Marcion*. In the former Tertullian is writing against the idea of an eternal cosmos, which would count as another god. In the latter he is writing against the idea of a god of creation and a god of redemption. In both cases he uses the criterion of divine monarchy against both propositions.

[15] *Against Praxeas* 3 & 4.

[Monarchy] has no other meaning than single and individual rule; but for all that, this monarchy does not, because it is the government of one, preclude him whose government it is, either from having a son, or from having made himself actually a son to himself, or from ministering his own monarchy by whatever agents he will.[16]

The point here is that monarchy focuses on the singularity of **rule**, not on the singularity of the **ruler** as the only one with any authority at all. A single rule can be organised in a number of ways (indeed, Tertullian includes the Monarchian suggestion as one possible way that in speculative human theory a monarchy could hypothetically be organised – his point is that this is only speculation and not what revelation shows).[17]

This throws the following question into sharp relief: if monarchy, whether divine or otherwise, is single and individual rule, and there are several authority holders within a 'regime', how do they relate to each other? The example Tertullian goes on to give is that of a monarch who associates his son in his rule.[18] This is obviously a very pointed example given the biblical data about the reign of the Son established by his Father.[19] Tertullian argues that the father in such cases does not necessarily himself stop being king or monarch. Of course, such association in 'sole rule' was not unknown in the Roman Empire.[20] But now that Tertullian has suggested some ways a sole rule could be organised with more than one person having authority, obviously we have to ask how far this could go and what sort of arrangement would undermine a monarchy.

3.3.2   What undermines Divine Monarchy

Tertullian's explanation of how division of power could destroy monarchy runs like this:

---

[16] *Against Praxeas* 3.
[17] Tertullian argues that just because something in God **could** be 'organised' in a particular way, that does not mean it **is** so organised.
[18] *Against Praxeas* 3.
[19] Clearly the fulfilment in Jesus of the giving of rule by God in Psalms 2 and 110 is very important here. Note also Matthew 28:18; John 3:35, 13:3.
[20] Diocletian's settlement in the latter half of the third century depended on this, but the practice had also been there in the second century. Trajan and Hadrian, for instance, were both beneficiaries of being 'associated' in the rule of the empire when adopted by Nerva and Trajan respectively.

Overthrow of monarchy you should understand as [taking place] when there is superimposed another kingship of its own character and its own quality [*alia dominatio suae condicionis et proprii status*] and consequently hostile [*ac per hoc aemula*] when another god is introduced to oppose the Creator, as with Marcion, or many gods according to people like Valentinus or Prodicus: then it is for the overthrow of the monarchy when it is for the destruction of the Creator.[21]

There are two stages here. First, since Tertullian has been dealing with the concept of monarchy as a general concept, he begins with a general point: any monarchy (whether human or supernatural) is undone when there is another rule (*alia dominatio*) which 'stands by itself'.[22] Put another way, monarchy is destroyed when there is a rule that properly belongs to and originates with some-one else, what one might call an independent rule. Such a kingdom is a free-standing rule in that it needs nothing from another in terms of force or legitimacy: it is independent and underived.

Secondly, with this criterion in mind Tertullian goes on to the specific case of the divine monarchy. He makes the perfectly standard point that another 'god' undoes divine monarchy by being a rival to God and notably in his character as creator. The stress on God as creator is again standard fare in discussing divine monarchy. Since God is creator of all else from nothing by his will and not from necessity, he is sovereign over it.[23] Another god who did not owe his existence to God, or who conferred alternative existence on things undoes that monarchy precisely because he 'stands by himself' and has an underived rule which belongs to him[24]

This means that Tertullian has a concept by which to test whether or not a theology which sees the Son and Father as distinct beings can be consistent with divine monarchy. The test is whether a claimant to the title 'God' has a second, independent rule, which does or could rival that of the creator God. This test is a real test: not all accounts of 'divine'

---

[21] *Against Praxeas* 3. '*Aemula*' could also be rendered 'rival'.

[22] The roughly parallel phrases *suae condicionis et proprii status* both contain the same two ideas of 'one's own' (*suus/proprius*) and 'standing'/'establishment'/condition (*condicio/status*).

[23] Revelation 4:11 is especially important in establishing that the cosmos and God the Creator are connected by the Creator's will and not by an ontological connection which could give rise to pantheism or panentheism.

[24] Which forms part of Tertullian's case against Marcionism.

fathers and sons will satisfy it, since mythologies such as Hesiod's in ancient Greece or that appearing in the ancient near eastern text *Enuma Elish* would fail it. With this test in mind, Tertullian can move to the issue not of how the divine monarchy **might** in human speculation be organised but how God has revealed it actually is organised.[25] In general Tertullian stresses we must deal with God as he has shown himself to be, rather than what we think he could be.

3.3.3   How the Divine Monarchy is organised

Tertullian goes on to explain how the divine monarchy is organised:

> But as for me, who derive the Son from no other source but from the substance of the Father, and (represent Him) as doing nothing without the Father's will, and as having received all power from the Father, how can I be possibly destroying the Monarchy from the faith, when I preserve it in the Son just as it was committed to Him by the Father?[26]

The key point here is that of the Father committing the power of his monarchy to his Son. For Tertullian, the Son's authority has been delivered to him by the Father, and he does things by the Father's will. This is not speculative but rather biblical, Tertullian will argue, because this is drawn from Matthew 28:18 and John 5:19 and 22. This committal of the Father's monarchical power is linked by Tertullian to the handing back of power by the Son to his Father as set out by 1 Corinthians 15:24-28.[27]

This means that Tertullian can argue that the Son has full divine power (entrusted to him by his Father), but the one-ness of the monarchy is preserved and this is shown by the way power is handed back. This latter point indicates that the Father has not, as it were, abdicated the throne of heaven: he has not stopped being God.

Therefore, there is no *alia dominatio*, for all authority traces back to the one source who continues to be ruler. Tertullian's test for whether a monarchy has been subverted is when there is a rival claimant with an independent, free-standing rule. But if we ask the Son why he holds the power of the divine monarchy, he himself refers us to his Father's will.[28]

---

[25] Tertullian speaks of the *oeconomia* of the monarchy. Like *monarchia*, *oeconomia* is another loan word in Latin from Greek.

[26] *Against Praxeas* 4.

[27] *Against Praxeas* 4.

[28] This is a particular stress in John: 3:35, 5:19ff, 13:1ff.

The Son specifically denies that his power has its own standing independent of his Father.[29] Therefore the divine monarchy is upheld precisely because the Son asserts his authority is given him by his Father and is not free-standing. Moignt's summary is that since the Son's power has no independent origin, the monarchy is not destroyed.[30] Derivation is critical here, giving a certain patrocentricity to Tertullian's monarchy, for the Son's rule traces back to the Father. It should be emphasised that this is what the Son himself says in legitimating his authority.

3.4   Evaluating Tertullian and the Pre-Nicene defence

How helpful are Tertullian and his fellows and what do we learn?

3.4.1   Positively

Tertullian does try to synthesise the biblical data.[31] He strives to have a theology based on revelation. Three biblical themes are especially important here: the first is God's cosmic lordship in creation. This is well-taken. His second is that the revelation on earth tells us about a son. Since this is a reality and God does not lie, the Son really is a son which means he is a different person from his Father. A father is not his own son.[32] If a father is his own son, the 'sonship' has no meaning. The third theme is that the relation between Father and Son must be seen in terms of what is revealed to us, not what we might speculatively think it could be. For Tertullian and his fellow anti-Monarchians, this is put in terms of the will of the Father, because that is how the Son puts it. Equally, when the Son is revealed as a son, there is truth in that revelation: if he is revealed as son, then he really is one.

---

[29]   As we will see later, this is an indispensable part of Jesus' defence to the charge of blasphemy that has been levied against him in John 5:18.

[30]   Moignt 'Le Probleme' pp 352-3.

[31]   Notably in his engagement over the exegesis of John 10:30.

[32]   Tertullian argues this at length in *Against Praxeas* 10: 'A father must needs have a son, in order to be a father; so likewise a son, to be a son, must have a father. It is, however, one thing to have, and another thing to be. For instance, in order to be a husband, I must have a wife; I can never myself be my own wife. In like manner, in order to be a father, I have a son, for I never can be a son to myself; and in order to be a son, I have a father, it being impossible for me ever to be my own father.' This is an argument from relational co-relativity, where in order to be something (e.g. father or husband), there must be another person who holds the 'other end' of that relationship (son or mother). Arguments from co-relativity are also employed by Origen and in the Nicene period by Athanasius.

3.4.2   Negatively

However, the pre-Nicene solutions are not helpful in every regard. Tertullian himself apparently takes the identity of the Second Person primarily as 'Word'.[33] Son is something that apparently happens in view of creation. This sits uneasily with Tertullian's own priority on the revelatory value of 'Son' as disclosing the Second Person. As observed above, this is not at all the same thing as saying that the Son himself is created,[34] but it does mean that we start to look to 'Word' as the primary identity of the Second Person. This, though, does not reflect the balance of the revelation in the Incarnation. We may say Tertullian's centre of gravity is on the importance of 'Son', but this is not perhaps worked through with complete consistency and thoroughness.[35]

Perhaps still more seriously there is the fear that this kind of response to Monarchianism opened the door to just the kind of ontological subordination that Arius was asserting in the 320s. Thus, G. Lampe suggests that monarchy is an 'illustration' that opens the door to 'extreme subordination and at worst polytheism'.[36] This trenchant criticism repays attention. If one accepts that Tertullian and others do open the door to Arianism in their resistance to modalism, then there must be a sharp discontinuity between orthodox anti-modalist and orthodox anti-Arian theologies. Hence it is worth looking in a little more detail at Lampe's position.

Some caution is needed here. We can usefully distinguish three parts in Lampe's argument:

- one, that 'monarchy' is 'only' an illustration.

- Another, that monarchy leads necessarily, or at least very naturally, to extreme subordination.

- The third, that extreme ontological subordination did historically emerge in the reaction to Monarchianism.

---

[33] He is strongly drawn to John 1:1ff, not least because John 1:1 features strong assertions both of full deity and distinction on the part of the Second Person.

[34] Despite Giles *The Trinity and Subordinationism* p 62, who misses the subtlety of Tertullian's position.

[35] In this respect he may have unconsciously paved the way for Marcellus of Ancyra in the fourth century.

[36] Lampe, G W H, 'Christian Theology in the Patristic Period' in Cunliffe-Jones, H. (ed.) *A History of Christian Doctrine* (Edinburgh: T & T Clark, 1997) p 56.

With regard to the first, that monarchy is 'only' an illustration, this is a very bad point. Tertullian (and the Monarchians) are quite correct to see monarchy as a very significant biblical theme and, as the NT use (notably in Hebrews) of Psalms 2 and 110 shows, a critical salvation-historical theme.[37] The divine monarchy and its possession by the Son at the Father's commission is part of the biblical data to which we must give heed. Lampe's dismissal of monarchy as 'only' an illustration risks obscuring this. It makes divine monarchy sound as though it is merely something Tertullian introduces by his own judgment as an explanation of something else rather than something genuinely taught in the biblical texts and of which any responsible theology must take account. In fact, divine monarchy is exactly the biblical datum that falls to be explained. Further, Lampe's characterisation of the divine monarchy as 'illustration' carries the ready inference that God is not really the divine monarch. But if God is not the divine cosmic monarch, then one naturally asks whether he is then sufficiently sovereign to save. Denying the divine monarchy is not only ignoring a dominant theme in the revelation of God, but carries hugely undesirable freight with respect to God's ability to save.

With regard to the second and third points, Lampe certainly does have a point that Arians appealed to some of the great anti-Monarchians. The question, though, is whether it is the theme of divine cosmic monarchy that drives this appeal or whether other theological motifs are more significant in creating conditions favourable to the emergence of Arianism. Origen of Alexandria is especially notable here. He was certainly anti-Monarchian,[38] but part of his argument was that the Father alone is *autotheos* (God in himself) and alone is simple.[39] Certainly Origen also argued that the Son was divine,[40] and he is associated with the notion of the eternal generation of the Son, but the restriction of 'God-in-himself-ness' (*autotheos*) and simplicity to the Father does raise the question of whether the Son and Spirit are as

---

[37] Thus Psalm 2 decisively interprets the rejection of Jesus in Jerusalem (Acts 4:25-30) while Psalm 110 is in particular interpreted by Hebrews with regard to the kingly and priestly work of Jesus.
[38] See his *Dialogue with Heraclides*. The issue was testing the orthodoxy of the bishop Heraclides over his alleged Monarchianism. It is intriguing that the early church set such store on orthodoxy that the non-bishop Origen was called on to take part in the examination of a bishop.
[39] *Commentary on John* 1.22.
[40] *Dialogue with Heraclides* 128.

much God as the Father is.[41] Indeed, we note that Origen argued for the complex/non-simple nature of the Son in order to explain how a simple God could be the ultimate creator of a complex and non-simple cosmos. The Son to that extent functioned for Origen as a mediator between the First Person, who was simple, and creation, which was multiple and complex. The Son for Origen enabled us to 'negotiate' between a simple First Person and a multiple creation. This interface between simplicity and multiplicity was not part of other anti-Monarchian theologies. However in this use of the 'multiple' Son as a sub-creator, there is a close affinity, albeit not an exact parallel, with the Arian beliefs that the Father directly creates only the Son, who is then the direct creator of all other created things.[42]

For this reason, while we may grant that some elements of anti-Monarchian discussion may have created some of the conditions for Arianism (Lampe's third point), there are other – and more plausible candidates – than simply divine monarchy. We would therefore need to test Lampe's second point further. The relevant question is: 'In the anti-Arian debate, do the Nicene theologians move away from the Father's divine monarchy because of fears it is covertly but inherently prone to lead to ontological subordinationism?' We will find they do not.

3.4.3   Relevance

The work of Tertullian and other anti-Monarchians is of enduring value today, and not just in setting the context for the Arian-Nicene debates of the fourth century. Apart from anything else, modalism is still with us.[43] More broadly, we are reminded that the monotheism/divine cosmic monarchy question is an enduring biblical question: we have to provide an account of Trinitarian relations that upholds these biblical values. Further, we see the importance of the creator-created distinction: Tertullian's final test for whether the divine monarchy has been divided

---

[41] Compare A Grillmeier's comments on this difference: *Christ in Christian Tradition* (Vol 1) 2 rev. ed. Trans. Bowden, J. (London/Oxford: Mowbrays, 1975) p 165.

[42] In turn, Origen's account may at this point owe something to creation accounts in Plato's *Timaeus*, where we see again the motif of a cosmic Demiurge who establishes sub-creators to carry out aspects of creation.

[43] Notably, for instance in One-ness Pentecostalism. For some K Barth tragically has very significant modalist tendencies, owing to his misconstrual of a concept from Anselm. See M Ovey 'A Private Love? Karl Barth and the Triune God' pp 198-231 in *Engaging with Barth: Contemporary Evangelical Critiques* (Nottingham: Apollos, 2008). Given Barth's modalising propensity, it is unfortunate that Giles *The Trinity and Subordinationism* places such store on his Trinitarian exposition.

is whether an alternative independent creator has been proposed.[44] This means that for the present question, (whether the Son's eternal subordination should be denied), the Tertullian question would be whether, if we do deny that subordination, the Son's power then becomes one which 'stands by itself'. If the Son's power does become a power that 'stands by itself', then divine monarchy has been subverted.

The anti-Monarchian solution to these questions is to work through what it means to have a revelation of the Second Person as son. As son, he cannot be the same person as his father. Further, the revelation principle means that the contours of that father-son relationship will be as they are revealed in the Incarnation, not as we might speculate they could be. This means that from the point of view of method, the anti-Monarchians make us ask: 'what is the kind of sonship that is revealed to us?' We will find that the Nicene theologians also work with this kind of principle – what is it for the Son to be son in the way the Bible reveals it.

Finally we need to consider how the anti-Monarchian approach of Tertullian and others fits with both the lines of argument produced against the eternal subordination of the Son (namely, that the Son does not obey at all and that he only obeys in his humanity).

The answer is 'very poorly'.

After all, the anti-Monarchian approach we have looked at stresses the Father's divine cosmic monarchy which he commits to his Son. This clearly does not fit with the Moltmann idea we have seen earlier that precludes authority.[45] Moltmann would naturally argue that this is simply a mistake by patristic theologians and we need to examine the substantive merits of his claim later, irrespective of whether or not it has patristic support.

But what of the other argument to the effect that the Son only obeys in the Incarnation? Does this fit? It would seem not, for this reason: Tertullian and others face the task of explaining how the divine cosmic monarchy remains intact **outside** the Incarnation. The thrust of the Monarchian challenge is that if the rule is divided outside the

---

44 See the passage cited earlier from *Against Praxeas* 3: '... **then** it is for the overthrow of the monarchy **when** it is for the destruction of the Creator.' [emphasis added]

45 We recall the quotation cited earlier: 'In this kingdom God is not the Lord; he is the merciful Father. In this kingdom there are no servants; there are only God's free children. In this kingdom what is required is not obedience and submission it is love and free participation.' Moltmann *The Trinity and the Kingdom of God* p 70.

Incarnation, then the divine cosmic monarchy is undermined and so is monotheism. If one confines obedience and submission to the Incarnation so that the Son does not receive his divine rule from the Father, then the Monarchian challenge is still unanswered. We would still be asking how the Son's own rule is not an independent free-standing rule that undermines the Father's.

For the arguments of Tertullian and others to work as refutations of Monarchian modalism, they must apply to the relationship between Father and Son outside the Incarnation. They are clearly intended to do so, since Tertullian naturally envisages just this as he sees the Word creating at the Father's behest, indeed, at the Father's command. To state the obvious, the Son's involvement in creation cannot be by virtue of his human nature. Creation pre-dates the incarnation of the Son at Bethlehem. Tertullian meditates on creation and the narrative of Genesis 1. He points to the repeated structure in which God speaks 'let us...' and then makes this comment:

> ...[T]hen you have two Beings – One that commands that the thing be made, and the Other that executes the order and creates.[46]

Clearly the work of creation, which Tertullian represents as one divine personal entity fulfilling the command of another divine personal entity, takes place outside the Incarnation.[47] We note also that, as against Giles, Tertullian depicts the Son as creator rather than created.[48] Hence arises the conclusion that Tertullian's divine monarchy argument fits poorly with the view that the Son only obeys in the Incarnation.

This all means that if the argument that the Son only obeys in his human nature is to be accepted, one still has to find an explanation for the continuing unity of the divine monarchy outside the Incarnation. The anti-Monarchians like Tertullian find this in the gift of monarchy to the Son by the Father and the reign of the Son in creation on his Father's instruction. It is not fanciful to envisage that the anti-Monarchians would naturally ask whether alternative explanations of the divine monarchy, for example as shared fully between three equal friends, are not essentially speculative since they move beyond what the Bible reveals. At best this would be superfluous in view of what the

---

46 *Against Praxeas* 12.
47 Nor is it a valid objection that this is inevitably an Arian account of creation: creation from nothing is what only God can do. To create from nothing, even if at the 'command' of another is still a divine action.
48 Giles *The Trinity and Subordinationism* p 62.

Bible actually does reveal and at worst would amount to proposing an alternative explanation as a substitute for what is in fact revealed. That clearly would be unacceptable and indicates that we must return to the content of the biblical revelation.[49] We turn now to the even more significant period, that of the Nicene-Arian controversy of the fourth century.

---

[49] See below on sonship in John in particular.

4   Nicaea 325 and Arianism

4.1   *The key Arian idea: that the Son is a creature*

If we are to consider whether the charge of Arianism has been rightly made in the present day, we have to ask what Arianism is. Arianism's key idea is that the Son is a creature, possibly a highly exalted and ultimate creature, but a creature nevertheless.[1] As we phrase the question in this way, we realise that again the issue revolves around what it is for the Son to be a son. Where Monarchianism argued that 'son' was compatible with Son and Father being the same person, Arianism argued that 'son' was compatible with being a creature of one's 'father'. Again, the issue is, 'What kind of son is the Son?' Arianism's answer is that the Son is created by his Father. Nicene theology characteristically opposes that.

4.2   *The Nicene insistence that the Son is not created*

This opposition to the idea the Son is created emerges in the original Nicene Creed of 325. This stressed against Arianism the status of the Son as son, not creature. The Creed reads as follows:[2]

> We believe in one God, the Father Almighty, maker of all things visible and invisible;
>
> and in one Lord Jesus Christ, the Son of God, the only-begotten of his Father, of the substance of the Father, God of God, Light of Light, very [=true] God of very [=true] God, **begotten not made** [emphasis added], being of one substance [*homoousios*, or consubstantial] with the Father.
>
> By whom all things were made, both which be in heaven and in earth. Who for us men and for our salvation came down [from heaven] and was incarnate and was made man. He suffered and the third day he rose again, and ascended into heaven. And he shall come again to judge both the quick and the dead.

---

[1]   Giles *The Trinity and Subordinationism* p 63 notes too the significance of the Arian claim that the Son is a creature.

[2]   The creed of 325 is not of course the same as the creed referred to in the *BCP* as the Nicene Creed. The latter is in fact the Niceno-Constantinopolitan creed of 381.

And [we believe] in the Holy Ghost.

And whosoever shall say that there was a time when the Son of God was not or that before he was begotten he was not, or that he was made of things that were not, or that he is of a different substance or essence [from the Father] or that he is a creature, or subject to change or conversion — all that so say, the Catholic and Apostolic Church anathematizes them [emphasis added].

For present purposes we must note several of the Creed's significant emphases: first, on sonship; secondly, the language of derivation ('of'); thirdly the terminology of consubstantial (*homoousios*); fourthly, that the Son creates; and fifthly, the key distinction between being begotten, as against being made or created.

The anathema section underlines the creation point: one must not say something that amounts to the Son being a creature.[3] Athanasius, who was after all an eyewitness to the development of Arianism, confirms the centrality of this question whether the Son is created. He describes the start of Arianism like this:

Arius and those with him thought and professed thus: 'God made the Son out of nothing, and called Him His Son;' 'The Word of God is one of the creatures;' and 'Once He was not'; 'He is alterable; capable, when it is His Will, of altering.' Accordingly they were expelled from the Church by the blessed Alexander.[4]

Against this both Athanasius of Alexandria and Hilary of Poitiers asserted that the Son was a true son, not simply a son by adoption.[5] Accordingly this means that the presenting question for the current enquiry is whether the Nicene theologians regard the eternal subordination and obedience of the Son as necessarily indicating that he was not a true son but a creature. If so, eternal relational subordination is Arian.

---

[3] The Council of Constantinople in 381, while it put the deity of the Spirit in terms of the principle of *homotimia* rather than *homoousia*, obviously did not resile from the 325 position that outlawed seeing the Son as a creature. After all, it retained the opening substantive propositions about the Son as 'of the same substance' etc.

[4] *De Synodis* 15.

[5] Athanasius uses true sonship phraseology at significant points, not just in relation to the Arian controversy: *Contra Gentes* 46; *De Incarnatione* 32, 48; *Contra Arianos* I.10; *Contra Arianos* II.5, 18 etc. Hilary uses it against both Arians and Modalists: *De Trinitate* II.4; VI.24, 27, 40; VII.6.

4.3   Summary of the Nicene Fathers Athanasius and Hilary

In fact, both Athanasius and Hilary use the true sonship of the Son to explain both the full deity of the Son and also how the divine monarchy and monotheism are preserved in orthodox Nicene theology. If the Son is true son, then he cannot be of a different ontological nature from his Father, since a necessary aspect of the father-son relation is that fathers and sons are of the same ontological nature (hence the Nicene term *homoousios* – of the same substance). Further, the Son's rule is by the gift of his Father and this is an undivided rule since the Son, like a good son, is subject or subordinate to his Father. The subjection or subordination of the Son plays a necessary part in showing how monotheism/divine monarchy is not undermined by the full deity of the Son.

4.4   The situation after Nicaea

As is well known, the Arians gradually recovered after the Council of Nicaea. In fact, with increasingly open and coercive support from the Emperor Constantius they were on the offensive,[6] culminating in a council at Constantinople shortly before Constantius' death which would have opened the door to Arianism.[7] This threat arose not least because of that council's prohibition on the use of 'substance' language, which had been hugely significant in delineating the boundary between orthodoxy and Arianism.[8] It became difficult to mark Arianism as

---

[6]   Constantius became joint emperor with his brothers on the death his father, Constantine, in 337. Initially ruling in the east he became sole ruler of eastern and western parts of the Empire from 353, following the assassination of his pro-Nicene brother, Constans, who ruled in the west. While he may have stood by when several members of his family were murdered in 337, there is no reason to think he was involved in the murder of Constans.

[7]   The Council of Constantinople 359-360. Constantius' death (361) and the rebellion of Julian in Gaul prevented full implementation of the Arianising programme.

[8]   This move had been foreshadowed at the earlier council at Sirmium in 357 which issued the document known as the *Blasphemia*. Before the meeting Constantius summoned in Constantinople, he had convened two other councils at Rimini and Seleucia (359-360), distinguished both by the coercive measures Constantius employed at those councils and their development of the theological themes established at Sirmium in 357.See below for a fuller discussion of Sirmium 357.

outside orthodoxy because the language to do this (that of 'substance' and 'consubstantial') was now proscribed.[9]

4.4.1   The parties

What made the situation from the 330s onwards much more complicated was the re-emergence of modalism (not infrequently referred to at this point as Sabellianism). A consistent concern was the extent to which the Nicene term 'consubstantial'/'of the same substance' (*homoousios*) had a pre-history which aligned it with modalism.[10] Notably, Marcellus of Ancyra was a voluble defender of the Nicene Creed of 325 but developed an increasingly modalist and Sabellian position precisely in his attempts to defend it. He was deposed because of this unorthodoxy on the modalist issue. Marcellus was initially welcomed by Athanasius, who was also in exile,[11] and by pro-Nicene Westerners in Rome.[12]

Hence the period after 330 is not just a struggle with Arianism: there are at least **two** major Trinitarian heresies on show in the period 330-360: Arianism and modalism. This is not always appreciated. Orthodoxy had to be asserted against both, and asserted in such a way that a refutation of one did not become a tolerance of the other, for example that a refutation of modalism did not over-balance into becoming pro-Arian.[13] Naturally, orthodox people might differ over which was the greater threat, and perceptions might differ depending on where one was in the Empire. This means that in the period roughly from 335 through to 360 we see not just Arians and pro-Nicenes but at least four somewhat confused groupings:

---

[9]   The issue from 357 onwards was not so much a straight, simple declaration of Arianism as of removing the terms by which Arianism could be declared heterodox: without the terms, Arianism could stand as a legitimate option within 'orthodoxy'.

[10] In particular Paul of Samosata, a bishop deposed for modalism ca 265, was thought to have used *homoousios* in articulating his modalist system and the term may well have been condemned in that context.

[11] But not deposed for theological unorthodoxy.

[12] This contrived both to snub easterners and sow doubts about where westerners stood. Athanasius was perhaps also at this point readily associated with Marcellus, which would not elevate his credibility in parts of the eastern Empire. Throughout his numerous exiles Athanasius retained a striking loyalty in the Egyptian churches.

[13] Thus, in the urge to refute the modalist exegesis of John 10:30 that the reference there means 'one person', some were close to saying the only reference was to a one-ness of will – that is, the Father and Son agreed. Of course, Arians could, and did, say precisely that. The issue is **why** Father and Son are at one. The context of John 10:30 makes us see that not only agreement but also mutual indwelling is in view.

- **Arians** (insisting that the Son is a creature and hoping to attract the non-Nicene group through a mutual fear of Sabellianism)

- **Sabellians** or **modalists**,[14] comprising notably, despite himself, Marcellus of Ancyra and, importantly, his protégé Photinus, Bishop of Sirmium. (Insisting that the Son is not a creature and seeking to make common cause with Nicenes through a mutual fear of Arianism)

- **Nicenes**, led notably by Athanasius of Alexandria and in the West from 355 by Hilary of Poitiers. (Contending that son and creature are mutually exclusive categories, and that as son, the Second Person cannot be a creature but equally, as son, is distinguishable from his Father. Suspicious of non-Nicenes on the grounds they are too open to Arianism)

- **Non-Nicenes**,[15] often associated with the East. (Not accepting Arianism, but not using the Nicene Creed as the formula of repudiation. Suspicious of Nicenes because of the welcome afforded to Marcellus of Ancyra and the fear of Sabellianism[16] – the non-Nicene position is probably best expressed in the Dedication Creed of Antioch 341, and the Creed of Sirmium I).

The achievements of Athanasius and Hilary, amongst others, were remarkable in this deeply confused situation. They both penetrated to the legitimate concerns of the non-Nicene groups which underlay their different terminology and found ways to persuade the non-Nicene groups that the best defence against Arianism was in fact the Nicene Creed, and that the Nicene Creed was not pro-Sabellian.

4.4.2   Creedal material 341 – 357

This is clearly a complex situation, rendered even more complicated by the increasingly overt and increasingly unfortunate interventions of the emperor Constantius from the mid-350s until his death. In those

---

[14] 'Sabellianism' is strictly speaking another version of modalism, taking its name from Sabellius, its apparent founder.

[15] The idea of 'non-Nicene' as a theological position that is not opposed to, but is independent of, the Nicene formula is helpfully used by Ayres, e.g. Ayres L *Nicaea and its Legacy: An approach to Fourth-Century Trinitarian Theology* (Oxford: OUP 2004), p 139. While independent of the Nicene formula, non-Nicene is not necessarily Arian. It might, of course, be *seen* as that, or at least as dangerously insensitive to the Arian question.

[16] The argument would be that if the Nicene Creed did not rule out the modalist Marcellus of Ancyra, then it must be defective.

circumstances it was perhaps natural that there were several attempts to outline a position which would safeguard orthodoxy from both Arianism and Sabellianism, and indeed some attempts by pro-Arians with imperial support to ensure Arianism was deemed orthodox. This in turn means we must examine some of the attempts in various creeds to safeguard orthodoxy. Remarkably, we find in this creedal material that Nicene, non-Nicene and Arian sources assert alike that the Son is indeed subordinate to the Father, and not just by virtue of human nature. We also find in Nicene and non-Nicene sources the vital assertion that the Son is a true son.

4.4.2.1   The non-Nicene Second Antioch 'Dedication' Creed 341

The circumstances surrounding the 'Dedication' Creed are important. The dedication in question was that of a new church, built under the auspices of Constantius. The westerner, pope Julius, had recently vindicated two important anti-Arian bishops from the east who had been deposed, Athanasius of Alexandria and Marcellus of Ancyra, and the talk therefore was of eastern toleration of Arianism. The bishops at Antioch derided the idea that they followed Arius and set out what they do believe, including this statement where the baptismal formula of Matthew 28:19 is quoted:[17]

> ....our Lord Jesus Christ ordained His disciples, saying, Go ye, and teach all nations, baptizing them in the name of the Father, and of the Son, and of the Holy Ghost, manifestly, that is, of a Father who is truly Father, and clearly of a Son who is truly Son, and a Holy Ghost who is truly a Holy Ghost, these words not being set forth idly and without meaning, but carefully signifying the Person, and order [translating *ordo* in Hilary *De Synodis* 29 and τάξις in Athanasius *De Synodis* 23], and glory of each of those who are named, to teach us that they are three Persons, but in agreement one.[18]

While the Antioch Creed does not use *homoousios* (consubstantial) language it nevertheless still does distance itself from Arianism. Hence its description as non-Nicene rather than Arian. It demonstrates its anti-Arian stance in several ways:

• it asserts the Son is not subject to change;

---

17   Several creedal declarations were made at Antioch. The second proved to be rather more significant.

18   Hilary *De Synodis* 29.

- there is not a time before he was begotten;

- and, a decisive anti-Arian moment, the Son is not 'a creature like the creatures'.[19]

These closely echo the notes struck by the anathema section of the original 325 Nicene Creed. That anathema section, of course, was laying out some particular ways in which Arian-style thought would assert the Son was a creature. In fact, in this creed, far from being a creature, the Son is said to be creator, the one by whom all things are made, associating him with creation from nothing. This is highly significant since to create from nothing is a divine prerogative. He is said to do the will of his Father, quoting John 6:38, but it is not clear whether this is restricted to the Incarnation or not. What is clear finally is the assertion that the revealed words 'Father' and 'Son' do have real meaning – they truly are these things. Here the creed is very close to the vital Nicene idea that the Son is a true son.

4.4.2.2   The pro-Nicene Encyclical of Serdica 343

Interestingly the pro-Nicene Encyclical picks up the theme of true son as it insists 'We teach him as true Son ...'[20] Given that the delegates at the Encyclical remained suspicious of the theological position of non-Nicene easterners, it is significant that true sonship really is common ground between the Encyclical and the Dedication Creed: the words 'father' and 'son' mean something. The Encyclical, though, also adds:

> None (of us) ever denies the statement: 'The Father is greater than I' [John 14:28] – but that does not apply to another hypostasis or any difference but (only) because the name of the Father is in itself greater than that of the Son.[21]

The Encyclical has been criticised for being overly brief on this point. However it does pick up on a favourite Arian text (John 14:28),[22] and sees in the relationship between the two Persons connoted by the 'names' (or terms) 'Father' and 'Son' an explanation of why the Father is

---

[19]   That said, a casuistic Arian might say that the Son was a creature but not like the creatures, that he was a unique creature and not like them in that sense. The wording is not entirely watertight.

[20]   Using the text and translation of Dünzl *A Brief History of the Doctrine of the Trinity in the Early Chucrh* (London/New York: T & T Clark, 2007) p 82. Dünzl is relying on the text and German translation of J Ulrich, *Die Anfänge der abendländischen Rezeption des Nizänums* (Berlin and New York: PTS, 1994).

[21]   Dünzl *A Brief History* p 83.

[22]   Arians argued that the Father was greater because ontologically superior.

greater. The Encyclical is thoroughly concerned to uphold the Son's full deity, but does concede that the biblical data shows there is some sense in which the Father is greater than the Son. Rather than explain the Father's quality of being greater by reference purely to the humanity that the Son has assumed, it locates this in the extra-incarnate relationship of Father and Son. In other words, its position on the way the Father is greater than the Son fits poorly both with Moltmann's relational egalitarian approach and with the argument that the Father's superiority is to be explained purely by reference to the Son's human nature. Instead Serdica links the Father's superior greatness to the fact of the Son being a son and the significance of the 'name' son. It explains the Father as greater than the Son with reference to their eternal relations as Persons.

Later pro-Nicene sources likewise stress the significance and reality of the 'names', or in more contemporary terms, the relational identities those terms reveal.

4.4.2.3   The non-Nicene Macrostich ('Long-Lined' Creed) 345

However, easterners were bound to be suspicious of a document in which Marcellus of Ancyra had been involved,[23] and it is thus no surprise to find the easterners producing another document of their own. This takes us to the Macrostich.

The fourth anathema of the Macrostich condemns those who say 'that Christ is not God'. This strongly suggests that we must see the Macrostich as non-Nicene rather than pro-Arian.[24] However, the supporting reasoning repays attention because of the way it clarifies that being God involves being eternal. The commentary on the anathema states:

> For we acknowledge, that **though He be subordinate to His Father and God** [emphasis added],[25] yet, being before ages begotten of God, He is God perfect according to nature and true, and not first man and then God, but first God and then becoming man for us, and never having been deprived of being.

And later the Macrostich states:[26]

---

[23] Some elements of the Encyclical do seem to have Marcellus' 'fingerprints' on them.
[24] This slightly cautious language is required because some Arians might indeed insist the Son is God – but only in a limited sense.
[25] In Athanasius *De Synodis* 26 the phrase is '...ὑποτέτακται τῷ πατρί καὶ θεῷ.
[26] Commentary on the seventh anathema which condemns those who say 'that the Son is Ingenerate; or that the Father begat the Son, not by choice or will'.

Believing then in the All-perfect Triad, the most Holy, that is, in the Father, and the Son, and the Holy Ghost, and calling the Father God, and the Son God, yet we confess in them, not two Gods, but one dignity of Godhead, and one exact harmony of dominion, **the Father alone being Head over the whole universe wholly, and over the Son Himself, and the Son subordinated to the Father** [emphasis added][27] but, excepting Him, ruling over all things after Him which through Himself have come to be, and granting the grace of the Holy Ghost unsparingly to the saints at the Father's will. For that such is the account of the Divine Monarchy towards Christ, the sacred oracles have delivered to us.[28]

Of course, some might argue that this language of subordination is only to be expected of a crypto-Arian document. This, though, by no means does full justice to the Macrostich. The Macrostich does concede subjection or subordination but refuses to move from there to the proposition that therefore the Son cannot be God but must be created. This means the Macrostich refuses the key Arian proposition that if one obeys, one must be ontologically inferior. Rather, as we have seen, the Son is eternal ('never having been deprived of being').

The Macrostich is, perhaps, not a perfect refutation of Arianism, but it does want to uphold key aspects of anti-Arian teaching, especially the flagship point that the Son is not created,[29] as well as other issues such as the Son not being subject to change, and there never being a time 'when he was not'.[30] Again, what is denied resembles the anathema section of the 325 Nicene Creed. In other words, the Macrostich asserts the Son is uncreated, unchanging and eternal: this sits very poorly with Arianism. But clearly, the Macrostich does explicitly state the Son's subordination, and, importantly, a subordination that is not confined to the Incarnation.

4.4.2.4 The non-Nicene but anti-Sabellian 1st Creed of Sirmium 351 (Sirmium I)

It is important not to confuse the creed produced at Sirmium I (351) with the creed produced at the later Sirmium II (357), as Giles

---

[27] The phrase '...*and the Son subordinated to the Father...*' translates '...τοῦ δὲ υἱοῦ ὑποτεταγμένου τῷ πατρί. Athanasius De Synodis 26.
[28] We note the language that the Father is head over the Son, but space precludes a full dealing with this. Suffice it to say that 'headship' language is thus not utterly unknown in the context of the Arian debates.
[29] See especially the commentary on the 7th anathema: De Synodis 26.
[30] Athanasius De Synodis 26.

apparently does,[31] given their very different contexts, contents and theologies. Factors such as the completely different texts of the two creeds, as well as the time difference between them of several years, not to mention the way contemporaries such as Athanasius and Hilary consistently treat the two as distinct all indicate that we should not conflate the two as Giles seems to. The apparent presenting issues behind Sirmium 351 were not so much Arianism as the resurgent modalism of Photinus, bishop of the important imperial city of Sirmium.[32] The 17th anathema of Sirmium I reads:[33]

> 'If any man says that the Lord and the Lord, the Father and the Son are two Gods, because of the aforesaid words: let him be anathema. **For we do not make the Son the equal or peer of the Father, but understand the Son to be subject** [emphasis added].[34] For He did not come down to Sodom without the Father's will, nor rain from Himself but from the Lord, to wit by the Father's authority; nor does He sit at the Father's right hand by His own authority, but He hears the Father saying, Sit thou on My right hand.

What is particularly in view here is the phrasing of Genesis 19:24, so that this 17th anathema refers to an act of obedience by the Son outside the Incarnation. This means that the strategy of suggesting that the Son only obeys in his human nature is not available as an answer to this instance of obedience. Nor does it help to say that the incident of Genesis 19:24 is wrongly explained as a Trinitarian reference. The reason is this. The point still remains that the framers of Sirmium I (and Hilary who comments on it) did not have any difficulty in asserting both full deity for the Son and his subjection to his Father.

However, we need to note the context of the 17th anathema. It is aimed at those who speak of two Gods. The declaration of two Gods might, of course, come about in two ways. First, the statement of two

---

31   Giles, K *Jesus and the Father: Modern Evangelicals Reinvent the Doctrine of the Trinity* (Grand Rapids: Zondervan, 2009) p 204/location 5324, fn. 111. See below.

32   Photinus was a disciple of Marcellus of Ancyra and Sirmium was significant because of its military importance in the co-ordinated security of the strategic border province of Pannonia.

33   Following Hilary's enumeration of the 1st Sirmium anathemata. The anathema quoted is numbered 18 in Athanasius *De Synodis* 38.

34   The phrase 'For we do not make the Son the equal or peer of the Father, but understand the Son to be subject..' translates Athanasius *De Synodis* 27: 'οὐ γὰρ συντάσσομεν υἱὸν τῷ πατρὶ ἀλλ᾽ ὑποτεταγμένον τῷ πατρί' And Hilary *De Synodis* 38 '*Non enim exaequamus vel comparamus Filium Patri, sed subjectum intelligimus.*'

Gods might be made by someone who really does want to envisage the Trinity not as one God but as two.[35] Secondly, this statement might perhaps be made by those mocking the traditional pro-Nicene and non-Nicene understanding by applying it to the exegesis of Genesis 19:24 to the effect that this is a reference to God the Father and God the Son. A pro-Arian might argue in a kind of *reductio ad absurdum* that on the non-Arian arguments one is actually left with two Gods. If one was left in this position, then the problem, the pro-Arian would continue, naturally, is that it would breach the two-fold principle of monotheism/divine monarchy. Therefore, the pro-Arian, would reason, the anti-Arians are wrong. However, the explanation in the 17th anathema is telling in the way it meets such an argument: there is no question of ditheism or polytheism and this is tied to the way that the divine monarchy is intact because the Son is subject to his Father. This, of course, recalls the kinds of argument Tertullian and others had earlier used to reject modalistic Monarchianism.

4.4.2.5   The pro-Arian 2nd Sirmium Creed (the Blasphemia) 357

The Sirmium *Blasphemia* of 357 ('Blasphemy') was a watershed. It clarified things.[36] R.P.C. Hanson's comment is deservedly well-known:

> It enabled everybody to see where they stood. At last the confusion which caused Westerners to regard Easterners as Arians can be cleared up. This is an Arian creed. Those who support it are Arians. Those who are repelled by it are not. [37]

We must remember that while the *Blasphemia* indeed opposed the Nicene formula,[38] it also stood against the non-Nicene Dedication Creed.[39] Hence it proved a litmus test on Arianism. The *Blasphemia*

---

[35] One might see this as a very gentle form of Marcionism.

[36] There may in fact have been few delegates at the council, but nevertheless the attendees articulated more clearly how the Arianism of the day articulated itself.

[37] Hanson, R. *The Search for the Christian Doctrine of God: the Arian Controversy 318-381.* (Edinburgh: T & T Clark, 1988) p 347. For similar evaluations of the Sirmium *Blasphemia*, see Ayres *Nicaea and its Legacy* p 137ff and C Beckwith *Hilary of Poitiers on the Trinity: from De Fide to De Trinitate* (Oxford: OUP, 2008) p 56. Key evidence for this view occurs in Hilary of Poitiers who notes that both 'eastern' and 'western' bishops were united in their condemnation of the *Blasphemia*: Hilary *De Synodis* 2-3.

[38] Evidenced starkly in its outlawing of discussion using *ousia* terminology.

[39] Hanson, *The Search for the Christian Doctrine of God* p 347: the Creed '...attacks [the Nicene formula], no longer covertly, but directly and openly, as it also attacks the Dedication Creed of 341.'

treated **both** pro-Nicenes **and** non-Nicenes as defective.[40] The relevant section reads:

> There is no question that the Father is greater. No one can doubt that the Father is greater than the Son in honour, dignity, splendour, majesty, and in the very name of Father, the Son Himself testifying, He that sent Me is greater than I. *And no one is ignorant that it is Catholic doctrine that there are two Persons of Father and Son; and that the Father is greater, and that the Son is subordinated to the Father, together with all things which the Father has subordinated to Him,* [emphasis added]....[41]

We can now see that the *Blasphemia* was not at all unusual in containing material relating to the Son's subordination: earlier pro-Nicene and non-Nicene documents have this too. Asserting the subordination of the Son outside the Incarnation is not a uniquely Arian position. We note also the use of the idea that the Father is greater than the Son, but – and this is critical – the sense that this is to be explained as ontological difference.

For what is unusual compared to earlier pro-Nicene and non-Nicene documents is to bracket the subjection of the Son along with the subjection of all things to the Father. This phrasing repays attention.[42] It suggests the Son is subject *in the same kind of way* as created things. This implies that in the creator-creature divide, the Son stands on the side of the creatures: the classic Arian position.[43] Typically, the association of creatureliness comes with the idea of subjection. This illustrates again the Arian presupposition that obedience and ontological equality are incompatible. Hilary also takes us back to the question of what kind of son do the Arians envisage when he summarises their position like this:

> .... They [sc. the framers of the *Blasphemia*] determined that God the

---

[40] 'Non-Nicene': using again Ayres' helpful term for a position that is independent of the Nicene formula, but does not repudiate it. Ayres *Nicaea and its Legacy*.

[41] As quoted by Hilary, *De Synodis* 11. Athanasius' account is found in his *De Synodis* 28 and differs little at this point. The phrase '...*the Son is subordinated to the Father...*' translates '...*filium subiectum...*' (Hilary *De Synodis* 11) and '...τὸν δὲ υἱὸν ὑποτεταγμένον τῷ πατρί..' (Athanasius *De Synodis* 28).

[42] See the very percipient footnote 5389 of the NPNF translation of Athanasius *De Synodis*.

[43] This is reinforced by the way the attributes of being without beginning, invisibility, immortality, and impassibility are predicated of the Father, but there is a pointed silence over whether the Son enjoys these.

Son should be asserted to be born not of God the Father, but of nothing.[44]

This usefully clarifies what is at stake in the continuing distinction or antithesis the Nicenes draw between 'begotten' and 'made'. If one is created, no matter how exalted one is, one's origin is from nothing, and if one is 'born of the Father' then manifestly one's origin is not from nothing: to be born 'of nothing' and 'of the Father' obviously exclude each other. If the Son is born of God the Father, then he is obviously not born 'of nothing', for the Father is not nothing. One cannot be born of two different kinds of things. Either the Father is father of the Son, or nothing is, but clearly not both.

Here, then, in the *Blasphemia* we have a subordinationist statement that is genuinely 'Arian'. This shows that the fears expressed by Giles, Carnley and others are not **always** groundless: some types of subordination are indeed Arian, but their Arianism consists in this crucial sense: that they treat the Son as a creature. His subordination arises from the fact that he is creature.

The next question is whether after the crystallisation the *Blasphemia* created, those opposing it would see **all** species of subordination as treating the Son as a creature. If so, they would withdraw from any endorsement of subordination, as necessarily tending to Arianism. Do they do this?

They do not.

4.5   *Responses to Arianism*

We will focus on two key pro-Nicene opponents of Arianism, Athanasius of Alexandria and Hilary of Poitiers.[45] [46] Both of them are committed to the true sonship of the Son, from which comes his eternal subordination, to which both hold. Some may ask why one should look at Hilary. After all, Giles 2002 does not mention him. Yet he was hugely significant in the defence of Nicene theology in the West of the Roman Empire, as we shall see, and is one of the few theologians

---

[44]   Hilary *De Synodis* 10.

[45]   On these issues the Cappadocian fathers uphold the priority of the Father, stressing like Athanasius that the cosmic monarchy belongs to the Father. The Son holds authority from him.

[46]   Some of what follows covers similar material to that found in M.J. Ovey (2014) 'True Sonship – Where Dignity and Submission Meet' chapter 6 in *One God in Three Persons* (2014) (eds. Starke, J and Ware, B.A.) Wheaton: Crossway.

Augustine names in his own mammoth *De Trinitate*. He was, of course, known as the 'Athanasius of the West', both in respect of his dogged courage (like Athanasius) and his defence of the Nicene *homoousios* Trinitarian theology. As such his omission by Giles seems odd.

4.5.1   Athanasius of Alexandria[47]

True sonship is fundamental to Athanasius' response to Arianism.[48] He uses true sonship to show that the Son is not a creature. For Athanasius, begetting and making/creating are mutually exclusive.[49] But Athanasius sees some differences between human sonship and divine sonship.[50] Is the area of filial subordination one of those differences?

No.

4.5.1.1   The Language Of 'Servant' Applied To Sons

First, Athanasius observes that the Bible applies 'servant' language to both human sons and the eternal Son. This is part of the biblical data that Athanasius has to explain. Giles 2002 does not explain that this is part of the 'task' Athanasius faces. Such biblical data had, though, been incorporated by the Arians into their argument that the Son was only a creature. The Arian argument here ran along lines like this:

> if the Son is a servant, as the Bible says, then he is a servant just like other servants (humans, angels et cetera). If he is a servant like other servants, and they are all created, then he, as a servant, must be created too, just like them.

Behind this lies a syllogism that goes roughly like this:

a) All servants are creatures

b) The Son (like other sons) is a servant

c) Therefore the Son is a creature

---

[47] Athanasius' response to Arianism is not, of course, simply after the Sirmium *Blasphemia*.

[48] Although his use of the idea is not restricted to directly anti-Arian polemic. As noted earlier, it is present in both *Contra Gentes* 46 and *De Incarnatione* 32, where it forms part of his account of God's restoration: there are salvific implications to the Son being true son.

[49] See e.g. *Contra Arianos* II.3, picking up the 'begotten not made' distinction of the Nicene Creed.

[50] For example, divine begetting is without sexual congress.

Athanasius has to explain this biblical data as well as the human usage by which fathers call their sons servants. He has to investigate what goes into proposition b) in the syllogism set out above.[51]

He produces his explanation as he addresses and defends the Nicene distinction between 'begotten' and 'made'. Can only those who have been made (i.e. created) be called servants? Athanasius argues that the usage of 'servant' is perfectly consistent with sons not being creatures made by their fathers because the 'servant' usage comes, he says, '... from their authority as being fathers.'[52] It does not imply difference of nature. Therefore Athanasius saw that a natural human father did have authority over his natural son. Obedience and authority do not necessarily imply ontological difference. This authority in the case of human sons as servants arises from the paternal relationship.

In fact, Athanasius' argument uses paternity in two ways: first, it allows him to assert identity of nature between begetter and begotten (humans beget humans ((not dogs)), dogs beget dogs ((not cats)) and God will beget God). This is one of Athanasius' key distinctions between 'begetting' and 'making' or 'creating'. If I make or create something it is not necessarily on the same ontological level as myself. I can make a cupboard, but I do not beget a cupboard.[53]

Secondly, paternity also allows him to explain 'servant' language as flowing from this same relationship. Paternity (begetting) grounds both the equality of nature and the servant language. In fact, it would be very surprising if Athanasius did not think along these lines. We have observed this pattern before in the way that a Roman son is by virtue of his sonship both a citizen and subordinate to his father. Similarly, with regard to descent conferring covenant membership and filial obligation.

Athanasius then meets the major point urged by the Arians to the effect that, like human sons, the Bible calls the Son a servant too.[54] He

[51] And ultimately has to show that proposition a) is false: just because all creatures are servants of God, it does not follow that all servants of God are creatures. The proposition 'all creatures are servants of God' is not straightforwardly reversible.
[52] *Contra Arianos* II.3. The word used for 'authority' is ἐξουσία. Giles *The Trinity and Subordinationism* p 39 fn. 23 does cite from *Contra Arianos* II, but does not refer to this passage.
[53] Athanasius sees 'making'/creating as an act of contingent will. For God to be Father is not an act of will like this, any more than he is good only because he contingently wills to be good. If we said he was good only because of his contingent will, then we would be saying he was not intrinsically, essentially good.
[54] *Contra Arianos* II.4.

argues that Solomon is rightly called both son by nature **and** servant of his father David because of a father's authority. As a son by nature, Solomon shares his father's nature (and derives his claim to inherit the kingdom). As a son by nature, he also obeys. Athanasius notes that if Arians find this acceptable in the context of human fatherhood, and do not think an obedient human son is ontologically inferior to his human father, then it should be equally acceptable in the divine Father-Son relationship. Athanasius' argument turns precisely on the parallel that exists between human and divine father-son relations over paternal authority. He thinks paternal authority is there in both human and divine sonships. It is vital to grasp this. If Athanasius were to restrict paternal authority to human sonship, he would not have answered the point the Arians were making.

Thus Athanasius accepts that relationships of authority between persons do not automatically imply inferiority of nature. Subordination between ontological equals is possible. For Athanasius, human sons are not inferior in nature to their fathers, even though there is authority, and the same applies in the Trinitarian relationship. This means that he rejects the Arian premise that obedience and subordination always preclude ontological equality.

Let us now turn to consider Athanasius' argument on this point as against the two major arguments used currently to deny the subordination of the Son. Is he consistent with them or not?

Clearly not.

Let us take up the argument that the Son only obeys in his human nature first. This is useless for Athanasius' purposes for the following reasons. For Athanasius to refute Arianism, he must deal with the relation of the Father and the Son **outside** the Incarnation. He cannot simply use the strategy suggested by Giles and others, namely that obedience language is restricted to the Incarnation. Athanasius is, of course, perfectly well aware of such arguments, for he ascribes other 'problematic' texts to the humanity of the incarnate Son. However, he conspicuously does not use this argument to deal with servant language applied to the Son. Why not?

The reason is not far to seek: the Arian case focuses on servant language applied to the Son **outside** the Incarnation. Giles' answer deals with servant issues **within and after** the Incarnation and so simply leaves the Arian case intact. Faced with Giles' response, Arians would be perfectly reasonable in shrugging and asking for an explanation of the point that they actually have made, namely of servant language **outside** the Incarnation. Giles' strategy leaves orthodoxy exposed to exactly the Arian challenge which he claims so exercises him.

Some might say that Athanasius is simply wrong to make the initial concession to Arianism and envisage that servant language is applied by Scripture to the Son in his relationship with the Father outside the Incarnation. This, though, again misses the point: even were Athanasius and Arians both wrong on this, so that there is no servant language applied by the Bible to the Son outside the Incarnation, Athanasius – the staunchest of anti-Arians – nevertheless still thinks that the Father's paternal authority is orthodox. He thinks that such authority is not necessarily Arian and that the Son's obedience as a servant does not mean he is a creature and therefore the Father's ontological inferior.

We must pass briefly now to the other argument currently used to deny eternal subordination, Moltmann's thesis that the relation between fathers and sons is not one of authority, whether the sonship is divine or human. This is clearly not accepted by Athanasius given the use he makes precisely of the natural authority fathers have in order to explain the use of servant language.

4.5.1.2   Bad Sons And Revolt

A second line of thought comes from Athanasius' observations about David's two sons, Absalom and Adonijah.[55] The context is Athanasius' refutation of the Arian charge that an uncreated Son would overthrow monotheism. Again we must stress the importance of the issue of monotheism as we analyse the arguments of the Nicene theologians. Athanasius comments on what David heard about Absalom[56] and Adonijah.[57] Both cases involve revolt from David by disloyal sons attempting to overthrow their father's kingdom.[58] Yet, says Athanasius, the Son is not like Absalom and Adonijah. The difference is that there is

---

[55]   *Contra Arianos* III.7 Again Giles *The Trinity and Subordinationism* pp 37-40 cites repeatedly from *Contra Arianos* III, but does not cite this passage which deals with what makes a good son.

[56]   2 Samuel 15:13.

[57]   1 Kings 1:11.

[58]   The 'overthrowing' is the common factor between Absalom and Adonijah on the one hand and the Arian charge on the other.

no 'rivalry',[59] nor has the Son called himself God and fomented revolt from the Father.[60]

We should note here that similar concerns arise as in the Monarchian controversy. If the Son is as much God as the Nicenes say, then why on earth is there not a rival cosmic kingship? Like Tertullian before him, Athanasius focuses on whether or not the Son can be seen as a rival. The issue of cosmic divine monarchy/monotheism is again in view. How does Athanasius establish that, while sonship makes the Son fully divine, this does not establish him in a rival cosmic kingship?

Of course, some might argue that an egalitarian relationship without subordination/super-ordination would ensure just such non-rivalry. The argument would run that the Father and Son as equals have an equal and total share in the divine monarchy by agreement between equals. Neither has a primacy, but each is equally entitled. A possible analogy would be that of an equal partnership under English law, where both partners may have equal voices in the conduct of the partnership's affairs and where the partnership progresses only on the basis of joint agreement, and not the obedience of one partner to the other. Obviously not all partnerships are equal partnerships, but some are and in an equal partnership of this kind it is clearly fair comment to say that there is no inherent subordination between one partner and the other, and yet such a partnership is not 'divided' but has a single principle of operation. This is a coherent egalitarian proposal for meeting the rivalry problem.

However, it is striking that Athanasius does not use this egalitarian reason. Instead, Athanasius explains there is no rivalry because the Son has glorified the Father and done his will,[61] appealing to John 6:38. So, for Athanasius, the Son is not a rival for his Father's throne precisely because the Son does his Father's will. This is a completely different rationale from saying something along the lines of a partnership analogy such as: *'there is no rivalry because the Son adheres to the mutually and equally agreed plans of Father and Son together'*. There is nothing in Athanasius' text to suggest mutual submission in an egalitarian partnership. Instead, the note of obedience is unmistakeable. Thus Athanasius uses John 6:38 to demonstrate the primacy of the Father's will by which the Father and the Son are so integrated together that the

---

[59] *Contra Arianos* III.7 ἄμιλλα, which can have the sense of contest for superiority, e.g. in a race.

[60] *Contra Arianos* III.7.

[61] *Contra Arianos* III.7 quoting John 6:38.

divine monarchy remains a monarchy. As he does so, he uses precisely the line of argument that those rejecting the eternal subordination of the Son argue he should not.

What is more, like Tertullian before him, there is a stress not on how human speculation might envisage the organisation of the divine monarchy, but on how the Bible reveals the divine monarchy is organised. Because the 'equal partners' model seems so obvious to us in the late modernist cultural west, we may perhaps forget that it is a legal model from our culture, albeit a powerful and congenial one, and therefore we may be over-inclined to answer questions on what seems 'obvious' to us.

We should turn again now to the two principal current arguments for rejecting eternal subordination. With regard to the argument that the Son only obeys in his human nature, this is insufficient for Athanasius' purposes. We recall again that Athanasius needs to repel Arian charges that the Nicenes have undermined the divine monarchy precisely with regard to the relation of Father and Son outside the Incarnation. He has to explain how outside the Incarnation the relation between Father and Son is not polytheistic. If Athanasius were to use the arguments of Giles and others, the Arian case would remain completely unanswered. While the Giles line of argument sees John 6:38 as referring to the Son only in his human nature, Athanasius does not, and cannot if he is to refute the way Arianism has put its objections. In fact, Giles specifically and somewhat surprisingly denies that Athanasius accepts John 6:38 as dealing with the Son-Father relationship outside the Incarnation.[62] The reality is that Athanasius has to use John 6:38 in exactly the way Giles will not accept. Athanasius has to use it with reference to the relationship outside the Incarnation, because if he does not, Arianism remains unanswered. What is more, Athanasius was right to read John 6:38 in this way, as we will see below.

There again, the use of John 6:38 to express the primacy of the will of the Father affirms precisely what Moltmann and others wish to deny, namely the existence of obedience relationships.

We should stress the way that Athanasius' reasoning here is in deep continuity with that of the earlier anti-Monarchians like Tertullian: the reason the Son is not a rival is because he does his Father's will. What the Son does are fully divine acts, but they are not independent or rival acts, but done in his Father's will. We sometimes think of Arians and

---

[62] Giles *The Trinity and Subordinationism* p 197.

Monarchian modalists as great foes, and there is no little truth in this. But there is an odd but important piece of common ground: both Arians and Monarchians employ the rivalry/divine cosmic monarchy line of argument to argue for non-Trinitarian solutions (ontological subordination in the case of Arians and modalism in that of Monarchians). But Athanasius' reasoning contains material to answer both Arians and Monarchians who argue that orthodox Nicene Trinitarian theology is polytheistic and denies the divine monarchy.[63]

Athanasius, then, recognises that natural sons sometimes infringe their fathers' sovereignty, 'unnatural' though that is. Such rivalry against a father is ethically condemned. Given the commands of the Decalogue, this is just what one would expect. By contrast, the Son is a good son precisely because he does his Father's will. This again, is just what one would expect, given the commands of the OT Law. Athanasius does not directly address the question of whether a son conforming to an egalitarian father-son relationship on the model of the 21st century cultural West would be a good son.[64]

Hence Athanasius did not see the Father's paternal authority as necessarily making the Son a creature. Rather he uses paternal authority to explain the biblical data, how a true son can be called servant, and is not a rival to his father. Paternal authority has a central part to play in upholding the divine monarchy and monotheism.

4.5.1.3   Responses to Athanasius' material on sonship

Naturally, this material from Athanasius is by no means unknown and the points developed above were recently set out. S. Holmes' response to the material reviewed above was to concede that it is 'more-or-less true' that a basic submission of the Son to the Father is taught' by Athanasius, Basil of Ancyra and Hilary of Poitiers.[65] But he adds 'there is more to be said about Athanasius'.

---

[63]   Athanasius' western contemporary Hilary of Poitiers makes much of just this point.

[64]   The obvious difficulty is whether this relational egalitarianism actually counts as fulfilling the Fifth Commandment, as expounded by Paul: Ephesians 6:1-3 and Colossians 3:20. See also 1 Timothy 3:4 for obedience in the children of presbyters, and Romans 1:30 for the association of rebelliousness towards parents with the disintegrative effects of sin. Jesus likewise upholds the Fifth Commandment in the dispute over corban: Mark 7:9ff and parallels.

[65]   Holmes, S. 2015 'Reflections on a new defence of "complementarianism"' http://steverholmes.org.uk/blog/?p=7507 (accessed 08.04.2016)reviewing *One God in Three Persons* (2014) The comments here on Athanasius and those recounted below on Hilary of Poitiers relate to chapter 6 of that book M.J. Ovey 'True Sonship'.

This calls for three comments. First, if it is 'more-or-less true' that Athanasius, Basil of Ancyra and Hilary taught a submission of the Son, then clearly that part of the charge against current complementarians that they have invented the submission of the Son is not true. It is perhaps unfortunate that Holmes does not draw out this consequence of his concession. Secondly, if Athanasius did repudiate the arguments he adopts here, then he would need fresh arguments to meet the points that the Arians made with respect to servant language being employed of the Son. It is not at all clear what those fresh arguments are. Thirdly, it is not entirely satisfactory to dismiss the material cited on Athanasius with the remark that 'there is more to be said': Holmes does not tell us what more there is to be said nor where we find it. Under those circumstances, it is difficult not to regard Holmes' remark as unsubstantiated.

4.5.2   Hilary of Poitiers

Like Athanasius, Hilary emphasises the Son as a true son of the Father. It would be fanciful to see Hilary as an Arian fellow-traveller. He wrote extensively against Arianism and was exiled in the mid-350s for opposing the Arianising bishop Saturninus of Arles.[66] By the time he completed his two great anti-Arian works *De Synodis* and *De Trinitate*, he had become familiar both with the positions of eastern theologians,[67] including non-Nicene theologians,[68] and had before him the *Blasphemia*. After his restoration from exile, he worked assiduously to rehabilitate the Church in Gaul from the effects of the Arian impact under Constantius.[69] As we have seen, Giles 2002 omits reference to Hilary and given the stature of Hilary's work, both as a writer and as a bishop, in the Arian controversy this seems perverse. In later works, Giles mentions Hilary in passing but largely with reference to his *De Trinitate*, not his *De Synodis*,

---

[66] Saturninus was Hilary's senior, but had proved remarkably open to Constantius' Arianising programme. It speaks well of Hilary's courage that he openly broke with the senior bishop for the sake of upholding orthodoxy.

[67] He had been exiled to present day Turkey.

[68] *De Synodis* is written at least in part to explain how the Nicene term *homoousios* can be properly used. In doing so, he addresses non-Nicene concerns about Nicene theology.

[69] Despite contributions in other directions, it is fair to say that his public anti-Arian position was the distinguishing feature of his career, including not just his opposition to Saturninus, but a savagely satirical piece against Constantius.

which is almost entirely ignored. This, as we shall see, is an unfortunate omission.[70]

4.5.2.1   Hilary's Reaction To Sirmium I 351

We have seen that the non-Nicene, anti-Sabellian Creed of Sirmium I (351) explicitly asserts the Son's eternal subordination.[71] If the arguments either of Moltmann or of Giles, Carnley and others were right, we would obviously expect Hilary to reject this violently. Does he?

No.

In fact, Hilary's commentary strongly supports Sirmium I in its explicit eternal subordination. He explains anathema 17 in these terms:

> God is One on account of the true character of His natural essence and because from the Unborn God the Father, who is the one God, the Only-begotten God the Son is born, and draws His divine Being only from God; and since the essence of Him who is begotten is exactly similar to the essence of Him who begot Him, there must be one name for the exactly similar nature. *That the Son is not on a level with the Father and is not equal to Him is chiefly shewn [sic] in the fact that He was subjected to Him to render obedience* [translating 'dum subditus per obedientiae obsequelam est'], *in that the Lord rained from the Lord and that the Father did not, as Photinus and Sabellius say, rain from Himself, as the Lord from the Lord* [emphasis added]; in that He then sat down at the right hand of God when it was told Him to seat Himself; in that He is sent, in that He receives, *in that He submits* [obsequitur] *in all things to the will of Him who sent Him. But the subordination of filial love* [pietatis subjectio] *is not a diminution of essence, nor does pious duty cause a degeneration of nature, since in spite of the fact that both the Unborn Father is God and the Only-begotten Son of God is God, God is nevertheless One, and the subjection and dignity* [subjectio ...et dignitas] *of the Son are both taught in that by being called Son He is made subject* [subjicitur] *to that name which because it implies that God is His Father is yet a name which denotes His nature.*

---

[70]   Giles, *Jesus and the Father* and *The Eternal Generation of the Son: Maintaining Orthodoxy in Trinitarian Theology* (Nottingham: IVP, 2012). In Giles, *Jesus and the Father* p 89/location 2022 he explains why he chose not to make Hilary 'a major debating partner': because 'it would have made each chapter too long, and...he is seldom discussed in the popular historical introductions to the doctrine of the Trinity.' Given the significance of what Hilary has to say on the issue Giles is examining, neither of these reasons stand up to scrutiny.

[71]   See anathema 17 of Sirmium I above.

Having a name which belongs to Him whose Son He is, He is subject to the Father both in service [obsequie subjectus] and name; yet in such a way that the subordination of His name [subjectio nominis] bears witness to the true character of His natural and exactly similar essence. [emphasis added][72]

It should be said here that Giles in later works is aware that Hilary writes about the anathemata of Sirmium I, for he responds to citations of it by P. Bolt.[73] His response though, as noted above, apparently shows that he has confused Sirmium I with the later Sirmium II.[74] It is conceded on all sides that Sirmium II was Arian. The former, however, was not. It explicitly opposed the foundational Arian positions.[75] It is therefore very unhappy that Giles dismisses the Sirmium I material as 'Arian'. That appellation belongs properly to Sirmium II.[76] The dismissal is singularly unfortunate since it seems to function in Giles' argument as meaning that he need not deal with the point that the text of Sirmium I actually makes: as 'Arian' it seems in his mind not to require any further consideration or answer, and in particular no consideration of the way that the anti-Arian Hilary positively endorses Sirmium I at this point.

More substantially, several points emerge from this anathema. First, the language of subjection, or subordination, and obedience is extensive.[77]

Secondly, the Son's subjection is theologically significant since it is employed to uphold the oneness of God. This implies that without the Son's subjection, divine unity is undermined. Again, we have to mark how significant the monotheism question is in the classic 4th century debates.

---

72 *De Synodis* 51.

73 Bolt, P. 'Three Heads in the Divine Order: The Early church Fathers and 1 Corinthians 11:3' in *RTR* vol 64 (2005) pp 147-161.

74 Giles *Jesus and the Father* p 204/location 5324, fn. 111.

75 The first anathema reads: 'But those who say that the Son is sprung from things non-existent, or from another substance and not from God, and that there was a time or age when He was not, the holy Catholic Church regards as aliens.' This reflects very similar anathemata in Nicaea 325, notably over the repudiation that the Son is created from nothing.

76 To be fair, Giles may have been misled by a faulty reference in Bolt 'Three Heads in the Divine Order' p 154, although to those familiar with the texts of Sirmium I and Sirmium II it is abundantly clear that Bolt is referring to Sirmium I.

77 Hilary's preferred vocabulary uses the *subicio* word-group to express these ideas.

Thirdly, Hilary describes the Son's submission as the 'subordination of filial love' (*pietatis subiectio*: literally 'the subjection of "piety"'). Obviously this echoes John 14:31 where Jesus links his obedience to his Father with his love for his Father.[78]

Fourthly, Hilary heavily stresses 'names'.[79] For Hilary, like other pro-Nicenes, the names are not mere titles but convey a reality. The name of 'Son' for Hilary indicates two things about the Son. First, as Son he is fully divine, but second it also brings a relation of subjection to his Father. This means that subordination/subjection is not something that precludes the Son's divine dignity. Both flow from the sonship. As Son, the Son has **both** dignity **and** subjection. It therefore opens up the further possibility that if one denies the subjection/subordination of the Son arising from his character as Son, one also undermines the grounds on which one says the Son is of the same nature as the Father. After all, true sons obey their fathers. And if the tell-tale sign of filial obedience is lacking, why think someone is a son at all?

Later material in *De Synodis* shows that this commentary on Sirmium I is not just a politically-motivated defence of a basically alien idea, but in fact reflects Hilary's own opinion.

4.5.2.2   Hilary's Own Confession In De Synodis 64

After outlining creedal material from others, Hilary articulates what he himself thinks:

> Kept always from guile by the gift of the Holy Spirit, we confess and write of our own will that there are not two Gods but one God; nor do we therefore deny that the Son of God is also God; for He is God of God. We deny that there are two incapable of birth, because God is one through the prerogative of being incapable of birth; nor does it follow that the Unbegotten is not God, for His source is the Unborn substance. There is not one subsistent Person, but a similar substance in both Persons. There is not one name of God applied to dissimilar natures, but a wholly similar essence belonging to one name and nature. *One is not superior to the other on account of the kind of His substance, but one is subject [subjectum] to the other because born of the other. The Father is greater because He is Father, the Son is*

---

78 *Pietas* is a key Latin virtue, not least for sons towards fathers. See above on the idealised figure of Aeneas in Vergil's *Aeneid* in this regard.

79 As had the earlier Serdica encyclical of 343.

not the less because He is Son. The difference is one of the meaning of a name and not of a nature. [emphasis added] We confess that the Father is not affected by time, but do not deny that the Son is equally eternal. We assert that the Father is in the Son because the Son has nothing in Himself unlike the Father: we confess that the Son is in the Father because the existence of the Son is not from any other source. We recognize that their nature is mutual and similar because equal: we do not think them to be one Person because they are one: we declare that they are through the similarity of an identical nature one, in such a way that they nevertheless are not one Person.[80]

By now, the position Hilary outlines is very familiar from similar statements from pro-Nicene Serdica, the non-Nicene Macrostich and the non-Nicene, anti-modalist Sirmium I. There is but one God, and both Father and Son are rightly called God. There are two Persons, as there are two names. There is, though, a distinction to be drawn between 'name' and 'nature'. The Father's superiority is explicitly not based on his being of a different substance or nature.[81] Rather it arises from the reality of the personal relationship, in which the Father begets the Son.[82] This is expressed through the terminology of the 'names', since the names betoken the personal relationships and personal identities. After all, the name 'Father' reminds us of the personal relationship that the Father has by which he relates as father to the Son, and similarly the name 'Son' reminds us of the personal relationship the Son has by which he relates as son to his Father, and so on. 'Superiority' is therefore not at the level of nature, a matter of ontology, but at the level of 'name', or of the Persons and how they relate to each other. The anti-Arian Hilary therefore does himself explicitly hold that the Son is subordinate to his Father.

4.5.2.3   The Importance Of The Subordination Of The Son For Hilary

Nevertheless, some might say that this position is fundamentally peripheral for Hilary. However, such an objection completely misunderstands Hilary's overall argument in *De Synodis*.[83] This emerges as Hilary unfolds his argument about the Nicene 'same substance' *homoousios* terminology. The Son's subordination is in fact

---

[80]   *De Synodis* 64.
[81]   'One is not superior to the other on account of the kind of His substance...'
[82]   '...but one is subject to the other because born of the other.'
[83]   Especially *De Synodis* 67-70.

part of his explanation of how *homoousios* is to be properly understood. This becomes clear in the following way.

Hilary knows one can use *homoousios* terminology wrongly.[84] Such wrong uses can nurture modalism. Given legitimate eastern fears about the western reception of Marcellus of Ancyra, this point needed to be admitted. Hilary then outlines how *homoousios* is rightly used.[85] To do this, Hilary has to show how *homoousios* does not open the door to modalism. Because the term *homoousios* could be misunderstood, Hilary stipulates: 'Let no one think that the word ought to be used by itself and unexplained.'[86] He moves on to what a proper explanation of *homoousios* involves:

> Let us bring forward no isolated point of the divine mysteries to rouse the suspicions of our hearers and give an occasion to the blasphemers. *We must first preach the birth and subordination of the Son [subjectio] and the likeness of His nature* [emphasis added], and then we may preach in godly fashion that the Father and the Son are of one substance.[87]

Hence for Hilary *homoousios* can **only** be properly taught in the context of the Son's filial subjection. For Hilary, filial subordination is not the fast track to Arianism, but actually **necessary** for Nicene orthodoxy. Hilary's account here suggests it would be tragically mistaken for those who want to defend the homoousios of Nicene orthodoxy today to do so by eliminating filial subordination. Eliminating filial subordination implies that the Second Person is not 'true Son'. This means that for Hilary filial subordination is not a trivial or peripheral position: it is necessary for a right understanding of *homoousios* which guards against modalism and for the Son to be a true son.

4.5.2.4 The Coherence of Hilary's Position

But does Hilary unintentionally let Arianism in, despite his best intentions, by defending the Son's subjection? Is his insistence that we need the subjection of the Son as a grounding for explaining *homoousios* simply a gigantic mistake on his part? A key question, then, is whether the Arian subjection the *Blasphemia* sets out and the Nicene subjection Hilary espouses can really be distinguished.

---

84 *De Synodis* 67.
85 *De Synodis* 69.
86 *De Synodis* 70.
87 *De Synodis* 70.

Hilary knows perfectly well that his position involves stating that both the Son and also all other things are subject to the Father. His point is that the subjections arise from different relationships:

A distinction [sc. between the Son's subjection and that of all other things] does exist, *for the subjection of the Son is filial reverence, the subjection of all other things is the weakness of things created* [emphasis added] [88]

Hilary's argument here turns again on the Son as son. Nicene theology, as we have repeatedly said, draws very heavily on the thought that the Son is begotten not made. Since he is begotten, the Son cannot be a creature. However, just as begotten-ness entails the Son's full deity, so it also entails subordination. Hilary has earlier emphatically linked begotten-ness with subordination.[89]

This means that for Hilary, the subordination of the Son is orthodox because it does not arise from a creator-creature relationship. Subordination does not necessarily imply that the Son is a creature. This is a genuine point of difference from Arianism which reduced the Son to a creature and in the *Blasphemia* sets out an authentically Arian subjection by bracketing the Son's obedience with the creatures. The Son and all other creatures, in Arian thinking, had a creaturely obedience. And since, the Arians observed, the Son obeyed outside the Incarnation and since (their key presupposition in this area) obedience precludes ontological equality, the Son must be a creature. However, Hilary has rather elegantly cut this Gordian knot by pointing out that sons obey not by virtue of the fact that they are creatures of their various fathers, but precisely because of the relationship of sonship. Fathers do not 'make' their sons, they beget them.

This line of argument allows him to reject modalism (true sons are different persons from their fathers), refute Arianism (true sons are of the same nature as their fathers, whatever that nature may be) and to uphold monotheism and the divine monarchy – the Son is not a second independent God with his own free-standing, underived rule.

4.5.2.5   Did Hilary Change His Mind?

However, much of this material comes from *De Synodis*. Holmes suggests that it is a mistake to see *De Synodis* as expressing Hilary's

---

[88]   *De Synodis* 79 'cum subjectio Filii naturae pietas sit, subjectio autem caeterorum creationis infirmitas sit.' Note again the use of *pietas*.

[89]   *De Synodis* 64, 67.

maturc thought.[90] Holmes does not in fact explicitly state that Hilary did change his mind from the arguments outlined above from *De Synodis*, but does indicate Hilary's thought changes and one possible implication is that Hilary changed his mind over eternal subordination. Naturally, this requires comment.

Hilary does indicate in Book VII of *De Trinitate* 'a change of mind'.[91] It is worth asking what this change of mind is. At the beginning of Book VII, Hilary recaps what he has argued, with no sense of changing the substance of what he says. He is concerned to uphold the reality of the name 'Son', insisting that because the Son is true Son, he is true God.[92] This is, of course, essentially, the same argument as he has produced before, and fits with both the non-Nicene Dedication Creed and pro-Nicene material. The change Hilary flags up is a change of plan of composition, not of substance, stating that he cannot deal as he had planned with the categories of name, nature, power and self-revelation as discrete units since the question of birth or begetting affects all of them. Birth or begetting is the key issue.[93] This closes a section in which he has stressed that with birth or begetting, what is begotten is of the same nature as what begets.[94] The name 'son' is true because the Son is begotten, and this guarantees the same nature as the Father.

All this, of course, is completely consistent with what has been said in *De Synodis*. This is scarcely surprising since the earlier material of *De Trinitate* appears to have been written very close to the composition of *De Synodis*, a point to which Holmes does not advert.

The heart of Hilary's argument in *De Trinitate* is in effect quite short. He writes:

> The Son draws His life from that Father Who truly has life; the Only begotten from the Unbegotten, Offspring from Parent, Living from Living. *As the Father hath life in Himself, even so gave He to the Son also to have life in Himself.* The Son is perfect from Him that is perfect, for He is whole from Him that is whole.[95]

---

90 Holmes (2015) 'Reflections'.
91 Holmes (2015) 'Reflections'.
92 E.g. *De Trinitate* VII.2.
93 *De Trinitate* VII.16
94 *De Trinitate* VII.13ff.
95 *De Trinitate* II.11. translating *Est Filius ab eo Patre qui est, unigenitus ab ingenito, progenies a parente, vivus a vivo. Ut Patri vita in semetipso, ita et Filio data est vita in semetipso. Perfectus a perfecto, quia totus a toto.*

What Hilary does here is in effect take Exodus 3:14 with John 5:26. Exodus 3:14 in Hilary's view tells us about a God who is utterly self-existent, with infinite life ('he who is'). He has explained how important this is,[96] and his point is that John 5:26 tells us that this quality of life ('life in oneself') is given by the Father to the Son. The Son has the same kind of infinite life as the Father, because that is what John 5:26 tells us and sons have the same kind of lives by nature as their fathers. This is the core of Hilary's position from which he works to other questions raised in the Arian debate. It is in fact soteriologically vital to Hilary in the way he describes the human predicament in *De Trinitate* I.1ff. Humans are subject to a finitude which renders life meaningless and only an infinite God can help: if the Son is not infinite, then he cannot save. This is more developed than what appears in *De Synodis*, but the idea of the importance of the Son being a true son who has therefore the same kind of life and nature as his Father is very much what *De Synodis* uses.

This takes us to the question of whether Hilary handles the subjection question in the same way in both books.

Hilary is well aware of Arian use of the Old Testament and therefore in Books IV and V of *De Trinitate* spends some time on the Son in the Old Testament. In particular this takes him to creation and the Angel of the Lord. Creation he regards as executed by the Son on the command or instruction of the Father. This preserves the unity of the created order and ensures we do not have competing creations by different gods. The Angel of the Lord he takes as the Son who is fully divine, but who has an 'office' to execute.[97] Hilary sees the Angel of the Lord in terms of Sender and Sent, which inevitably reminds one of the sending motif in John's Gospel. Hilary summarises thus:

> I have shewn also that the Law, gradually unfolding the Gospel mystery, reveals the Son as a Person by manifesting God as obedient, in the creation of the world, to the words of God, (*et in creando mundo oboedientem dictis Dei Deum*) and in the formation of man making what is the joint image of God, and of God; and again, that in the judgment of the men of Sodom the Lord is Judge from the Lord; that, in the giving of blessings and ordaining of the

---

96 *De Trinitate* I.5ff.
97 'The title *Messenger* proves that He has an office of His own; that His nature is truly Divine is proved when He is called God' *De Trinitate* V.11

mysteries of the Law, the Angel of God is God.[98]

The note of obedience by the Son outside the Incarnation is unmistakeable, and completely consistent with earlier non-Nicene and pro-Nicene handling of the OT question.

Moving to the New Testament, Hilary writes of the works of the Son in these terms:

> God the Only-begotten proves His Sonship by an appeal not only to the name, but to the power; the works which He does are evidence that He has been sent by the Father. What, I ask, is the fact which these works prove? That He was sent. That He was sent, is used as a proof of His sonlike obedience and of His Father's authority: for the works which He does could not possibly be done by any other than Him Who is sent by the Father. (*Itaque et Fili oboedentia et paterna auctoritas docetur in misso, dum alterius opera esse non possunt quae facit, nisi eius qui missus a Patre sit*)[99]

Naturally there is a clear similarity here to the thoughts of Athanasius on the way that a father has a paternal authority and a son a filial obedience.

Hilary continues to be insistent that the generation of the Son as son means both deity and filial obedience:

> Though He proclaimed one God the Father, He declared Himself to be in the nature of the one God, by the truth of His generation. Yet in His office as Son and His condition as man, He subjected Himself to God the Father, (*nec tamen se Deo Patri non et fili honore et hominis condicione subdente*) since everything that is born must refer itself back to its author, and all flesh must confess itself weak before God.[100]

P Smulders comments on this that the Son does not just submit in the nature he assumed (his humanity), but relates in this way as son to

---

[98] *De Trinitate* V.24

[99] *De Trinitate* VI.27.

[100] *De Trinitate* IX.5.

father.[101] Smulders notes this text does not stand alone in referring to the Son's filial obedience, citing also *De Trinitate* IX.53,[102] and XI.12.[103] This pattern of using the Son's generation from the Father to guarantee both full deity and a relation of obedience which is independent of that of a creature is, of course, familiar from *De Synodis*.

Hilary is concerned to uphold the reality of both natures that the Son has, the one he has from his Father and the human nature he assumes. He envisages therefore a two-fold pattern of relation, that the Son relates to his Father not just as Father in the eternal relationship but he also relates to the First Person as creature because of the humanity. The reality of both natures is certainly developed at much greater length than in *De Synodis*, but given the way that the Father's prerogatives as Father are consistently emphasised, this does not amount to a change of mind on the issue of eternal subordination, which is, after all, the point at issue.

A good example of the way Hilary envisages the Father's prerogatives comes in his explanation of Jesus' statement that he does not know the date of his return, but his Father does. For Hilary this is not because of the Son's ignorance, but because the Father is not yet ready to disclose it. He summarises his argument thus:

> ....and the Father reserves as His prerogative, to demonstrate His authority as the Unbegotten, the fixing of this still undetermined day. ... It is to demonstrate against the Sabellian heretics that the Father's authority is without birth or beginning, that this

---

101 Smulders, P. (2001) *De Trinitate* Paris: Cerf. Watson, Bennett, E.N. and Gayford, S.C. vol 3 p 23, fn 4, which reads 'Ce n'est pas seulement dans la nature assumée qu'il se soumet au Créateur, mais même dans sa naissance éternelle il reconnaît que le Père est son principe et il lui rend grâces de sa naissance par l'honneur qu'il lui défère. En tant que Fils, il donne la considération qu'il doit à celui dont il a tout reçu.' (quoting P Smulders (1944) *La Doctrine trinitaire de S. Hilaire de Poitiers* Rome: Universitatis Gregorianae p. 180,).

102 The relevant part reads: 'He pays to the Father the tribute of obedience to the will of Him Who sent Him, but the obedience of humility (*oboedientia humilitatis*) does not dissolve the unity of His nature: He becomes obedient unto death, but, after death, He is above every name.' *De Trinitate* IX.53

103 The relevant part reads: 'See in all that He said, how carefully the Lord tempers the pious acknowledgment of His debt, so that neither the confession of the birth could be held to reflect upon His divinity, nor His reverent obedience to infringe upon His sovereign nature. He does not withhold the homage due from Him as the Begotten, Who owed to His Author His very existence, but He manifests by His confident bearing the consciousness of participation in that nature, which belongs to Him by virtue of the origin whereby He was born as God.' *De Trinitate* XI.12

prerogative of unbegotten authority is not granted to the Son.[104]

Holmes refers to Book XII as another point where Hilary changes tack.[105] However Book XII shows Hilary centring on the implications of the Son being born from an eternal nature. This is relevant for the key question of whether the Son is a creature and what one is to make of ideas such as 'once the Son was not'. Hilary summarises like this:

> Therefore the conclusion reached by faith and argument and thought is that the Lord Jesus both was born and always existed. [106]

This is standard for Hilary and is reached by applying his standard thought that the nature of the begetter determines the nature of the begotten, and that the relations within the Trinity are co-relative. This is consistent not just with the rest of De Trinitate but with De Synodis too. From this Hilary goes on to deal with the Arian flagship text of Proverbs 8:23-4.

It will be evident from this that Holmes' implication that Hilary has changed his mind from the findings he made in De Synodis on eternal subordination has not been demonstrated to be true. Obedience language outside the Incarnation, arising from the begetting of the Son continues to be present.

Some developing features of De Trinitate do repay attention, however. First, Hilary wants to uphold the free will of the Son and wishes to assert that the Son does not carry out his works of obedience under compulsion. Secondly, Hilary approaches Arian arguments about the Son and Father being of one mind by agreement only in terms of the Father and Son by nature willing the same thing. These issues relating to the will of the Son are explored more fully below in the context of the dyothelite controversy.

The third feature that repays attention is the extensive use Hilary makes of Philippians 2 and the Son emptying himself. This is markedly a stronger motif than in De Synodis. In particular, Hilary is clearly struck by the humility of the Son in taking human nature and he relates this to obedience:

> But in the dispensation of the flesh which He assumed, and through the obedience whereby He emptied Himself of the form of

---

[104] De Trinitate X.8.
[105] Holmes (2015) 'Reflections'.
[106] De Trinitate XII.32.

God, (*per exinanientis se ex forma Dei oboedientiam*) Christ, born man, took to Himself a new nature, not by loss of virtue or nature but by change of fashion.[107]

Hilary is clearly concerned here to affirm that the Son remained fully divine during the Incarnation, and that he assumed another nature, having the '... [f]ull reality of each nature'.[108] Yet the hint here is that the Son assumes human nature because he is already humbly obedient – that is humbly obedient in his eternal relationships. He does not become humble in character because he has assumed a second, lower nature. This bears on the question of whether we should see humility as an eternal virtue of the Son or not. Did the Son take humanity because he was humbly obedient, or did he become humbly obedient because he had taken human flesh? This is developed further below.

On the whole, therefore, Holmes' implication that Hilary changed between *De Synodis* and *De Trinitate* on the question of the subordination of the Son seems not just unsubstantiated but contrary to the evidence.

However, we need also to consider briefly patristic authors who have been felt to take a contrary view to the filial subordination of the Son.

4.6   *Patristic Counter-arguments to Athanasius and Hilary?*

Naturally the question might fairly be asked whether all the pro-Nicene theologians reproduce the approaches we see in Athanasius and Hilary. In particular we should have in view the Cappadocian theologians and Augustine.[109] Overall, we do find some different strains at times in these theologians, but notably find the same continued concerns over the preservation of the divine monarchy and the reality of the Son as a true son.

4.6.1   The Cappadocians

4.6.1.1   Gregory of Nazianzen

We begin with Gregory of Nazianzen and his comments on John 6:38, which he explains in conjunction with Jesus' prayer in Gethsemane. We

---

[107] *De Trinitate* IX.38
[108] *De Trinitate* IX.3
[109] The Cappadocians are frequently cited at the moment as *chic* Trinitarian theologians, while Augustine is obviously of huge significance for western theology, although his Trinitarian thought has been associated with modalism, notably because of remarks by A Harnack.

have seen that Athanasius uses John 6:38 to explain how Jesus the Son is a good son outside the Incarnation, in contrast to Absalom and Adonijah. Speaking of Jesus praying that 'your will be done', Gregory says:

> But since, as this is the language of Him Who assumed our Nature (for He it was Who came down), and not of the Nature which He assumed, we must meet the objection in this way, that the passage does not mean that the Son has a special will of His own, besides that of the Father, but that He has not; so that the meaning would be, "not to do Mine own Will, for there is none of Mine apart from, but that which is common to, Me and Thee; for as We have one Godhead, so We have one Will."[110]

Two things are striking here. First, Gregory does not restrict the language of Jesus in John 6:38 and Matthew 26:38 to a reference to Jesus in his human nature. He stresses that the person who speaks is Jesus the Son.[111] Gregory does indeed use the argument from time to time that certain things are said in respect of the Son's human nature,[112] but does not do so here. Secondly, we must admit that Gregory's exegesis of Matthew 26:38 is deeply unsatisfactory.[113] It leaves unanswered some really very serious questions about the relationship between the will of Jesus the Son in his human nature and the joint will Jesus also has by divine nature with the Father and the Spirit. Put another way, the question becomes one of the inner coherence of the Person of Jesus the Son. In particular, Gregory leaves us asking whether, if the will that Jesus follows throughout his life is the common, numerically single will of both Father and Son, Jesus genuinely obeys in his life on earth at all. This, naturally, makes one ask whether he truly is the new, perfect Adam who does not fall. These considerations are more fully developed below as we look at the dyothelite controversy and why the eternal subordination of the Son offers the best way of preserving the inner coherence of the Person of the Son and his genuine obedience.

---

[110] Gregory of Nazianzen *Fourth Theological Oration* XII.

[111] Gregory of Nazianzen *Fourth Theological Oration* XII: 'Well, if this had not been said by Himself Who came down, we should say that the phrase was modelled as issuing from the Human Nature...'

[112] E.g. Gregory of Nazianzen *Third Theological Oration* XVII.

[113] D Bathrellos *The Byzantine Christ* p 141 notes it is 'problematic'. 'It does not take seriously the genuine character of Christ's predicament which is expressed in his prayer.'

To this extent, while Gregory does at times reflect some of the arguments that Giles and others have recently used, he still speaks of John 6:38 as dealing with the voice of the Son outside the Incarnation, and leaves unresolved the serious issue of the inner coherence of the Person of Jesus the Son. This means that for all Gregory's contributions to the development of Trinitarian theology, he does not on this point represent a better alternative than Hilary and Athanasius.

4.6.1.2   Basil the Great

We turn now to consider Basil the Great. Basil was, of course, highly instrumental in arguing for the deity of the Holy Spirit, proclaimed at the Council of Constantinople 381, on the basis of *homotimia*, the principle that the Spirit should be honoured equally with the Father and Son.[114] In the course of defending the deity of the Spirit, he writes this about passages in John which seem to speak of the Father instructing the Son:

> When then He [sc Jesus] says, "I have not spoken of myself, and again, "As the Father said unto me, so I speak," and "The word which ye hear is not mine, but [the Father's] which sent me," and in another place, "As the Father gave me commandment, even so I do," it is not because He lacks deliberate purpose or power of initiation, nor yet because He has to wait for the preconcerted key-note, that he employs language of this kind. His object is to make it plain that His own will is connected in indissoluble union with the Father. Do not then let us understand by what is called a "commandment" a peremptory mandate delivered by organs of speech, and giving orders to the Son, as to a subordinate, concerning what He ought to do. Let us rather, in a sense befitting the Godhead, perceive a transmission of will, like the reflexion of an object in a mirror, passing without note of time from Father to Son. "For the Father loveth the Son and sheweth him all things," so that "all things that the Father hath" belong to the Son, not gradually accruing to Him little by little, but with Him all together and at once.[115]

This passage repays attention for a number of reasons. We should note first the sentence:

[114] Expressed in the Niceno-Constantinopolitan formulation about belief in the Spirit '....who with the Father and the Son is worshipped and glorified...'
[115] Basil *On the Holy Spirit* 20.

Do not then let us understand by what is called a "commandment" a peremptory mandate delivered by organs of speech, and giving orders to the Son, as to a subordinate, concerning what He ought to do.[116]

Taken by itself this could suggest that Basil is simply denying any kind of subordination on the part of the Son. In fact the context shows his point is more subtle than this. He quotes some of the 'obedience' texts Arians used but then does not solve the problem by a straightforward appeal to an obedience that is restricted to the Son's human nature. Once again, a strong pro-Nicene does not use the argument that Giles and others suggest he should.

Instead, he explains that one must not understand the 'obedience' texts as indicating some kind of lack on the part of the Son (that he is without the power or faculty of deliberate purpose). The reason for this is not far to seek. Such a lack would open the door to two equally unacceptable alternatives.

- The first unacceptable alternative is that if the Son did lack the power of deliberate purpose in terms of his **human nature**, then we would have to say that he had not assumed full humanity, because humans do have such a power of deliberate purpose, even if we exercise it badly.[117] And as the Cappadocians insisted, 'the unassumed is the unhealed'. In other words if the Son did not assume complete human nature then not all of human nature has been redeemed in us. This is why this alternative is unacceptable.

- The other unacceptable alternative is that Jesus the Son has no power of deliberative purpose in his **divine nature**. This is clearly lethal in the context of the Arian debate, since this would mean that Jesus the Son did not have the whole of the divine nature. As such he could not be fully God. As such we would either be left with a graded polytheism, rather like some species of paganism, or with the simple confession that Jesus the Son is not 'true God', contrary to the insistence of the Nicene Creed.

For these reasons, Basil argues, one must emphatically not see the obedience texts as indicating some kind of lack on the part of the Son. Rather, Basil explains Jesus' purpose in these texts like this: 'His [sc.

---

[116] Basil *On the Holy Spirit* 20.
[117] Such an account of an incomplete human nature assumed by the Son was proposed by Apollinarius during this period.

Jesus] object is to make it plain that His own will is connected in indissoluble union with the Father.'[118] This means that Basil is concerned to ensure that any exegesis of the obedience texts must not create a disjunction between the wills of Father and Son: their wills are in 'indissoluble union'.[119] This 'indissoluble union' means that there can be no time gap ('without note of time') between Father and Son as the former orders and the latter executes.[120]

This issue of time gap is more important than we might at first think. If there were a time gap then the fear no doubt is that this would introduce time and succession into the Son. To a theologian like Basil who is strongly committed to the transcendence of God this is a dangerous line to go down. For if the Son is subject to time and succession this would make him less than eternal but rather subject to change, and, as the anathemata of the 325 Nicene Creed state, the Son is not subject to change. To this extent, the time gap would undermine the full deity of the Son, and hence cannot be contemplated: time and succession, so to speak, are for creatures.

The next consideration that arises from Basil's term 'indissoluble union' is that this is not necessarily making quite the same point as Gregory of Nazianzen does with respect to the will of Father and Son in the Gethsemane prayer. There Gregory speaks in terms of '...We have one Will."[121] This phrasing suggests one common, numerically single will between Father and Son, not just two wills that are perfectly aligned.[122] But Basil's phrasing of 'indissoluble union' suggests rather two wills numerically between Father and Son but which are so closely joined that they are indissoluble and cannot be separated. A 'union' suggests two items joined, rather than just one single item. To this extent, the Cappadocians may differ as between themselves.[123]

This means the following for the present debate about the eternal subordination of the Son. First, Basil reminds us that the eternal subordination of the Son cannot be put in a way that implies a lack on the part of the Son either as human or as God. In particular, a

---

[118] Basil *On the Holy Spirit* 20.
[119] The term 'will' does not necessarily bear at this point the highly technical meaning it came to have in the debates about dyothelitism with Maximus the Confessor.
[120] Basil *On the Holy Spirit* 20.
[121] Gregory of Nazianzen *Fourth Theological Oration* XII.
[122] The comparison between the one Godhead and the one will suggests this too.
[123] Obviously it is possible to over-estimate the extent to which the Cappadocians agreed with each other.

disjunction based on time or ignorance between the wills of Father and Son cannot be accepted. Rather the 'indissoluble union' of their wills must be upheld. This usefully reminds us that the subordination of the Son can be put in a way that is unacceptable. Arianism classically suggested that the subordination arises from the fact that the Son was a creature, and here Basil objects to a subordination based on any defect or lack in the Son in terms of will: after all, such a lack would mean there is no 'indissoluble union' of wills and that would undermine the equal but monotheistic deity of the Son.

This means secondly that Basil is not rejecting all and any version of subordination – rather a subordination put in a way that means the Son is subordinate in a creaturely way: any subordination must be based on an 'indissoluble union' of wills. This is equally true, of course, of an egalitarian account of the eternal relation between Father and Son. The egalitarian dialogue between Father and Son must not be thought of as involving ignorance or succession or time gap or anything that would detract from the full deity of both Persons.

4.6.1.3   Cappadocian Concerns

Given what we have seen above we may start to wonder how different the Cappadocians are in principle from Athanasius and Hilary. Certainly we should remark on the following concerns over the proclamation of the deity of the Son.

First, as with the pre-Nicenes and Athanasius and Hilary, there is a key commitment to the divine monarchy as a theological foundation. Gregory of Nazianzen elegantly summarises:

> The three most ancient opinions concerning God are Anarchia, Polyarchia, and Monarchia. The first two are the sport of the children of Hellas, and may they continue to be so. For Anarchy is a thing without order; and the Rule of Many is factious, and thus anarchical, and thus disorderly. For both these tend to the same thing, namely disorder; and this to dissolution, for disorder is the first step to dissolution. But Monarchy is that which we hold in honour. It is, however, a Monarchy that is not limited to one Person...[124]

At this point we have a very similar note being struck to Tertullian: there is a single rule but more than one Person is associated in that

---

[124]   Gregory *Third Theological Oration* II.

rule. Further, the Cappadocians, like their predecessors and contemporaries, see a priority for the Father here. The Son fully shares in the rule, but the Father is the Source of it.

This takes us to the second concern. If the Son is fully God he must be honoured with equal honour. This comment from Gregory of Nazianzen is highly illuminating:

> ...and then you [sc. The Arians] ascribe this Name [sc. God] to the Father, while you deprive the Son of it, and make Him subject to the Father, and give Him only a secondary honour and worship.[125]

Gregory's point here is that Arians do not accept the Son as truly God but reserve that for the Father, who correspondingly is worshipped with higher honour. It is in this sense that the Son is subjected to the Father. This is perceptive since it is a reminder that if eternal subordination is put in a way that means the Son is not worshipped as fully divine, then that formulation cannot be right. The question then is whether the eternal subordination of the Son must necessarily mean that the Father is 'entitled' to higher honour than the Son.

This, though, in turn raises questions about how we value humility and obedience. There is a genuine question as to whether we think one who humbly obeys is worthy of less honour than one who does not but exercises authority. If we do indeed see humility and obedience as general moral virtues, a part of 'goodness', then naturally we will be inclined to think that far from being a litmus test that shows 'second order' deity, the eternal subordination of the Son is itself something for which he should be honoured and worshipped. However, we must defer prolonged discussion until the theological section of this monograph. Suffice it to say here that if our working principle is that the less subordinate one is, the more one should be honoured, then we are getting close to the worship of power alone.

This takes us to the third area of concern for the Cappadocians. We have mentioned their principle that the Father is the Cause (*Aitia*) or Beginning of the Trinity.[126] Certainly the Cappadocians wanted to give due weight to the biblical data and that data notably included John 14:28 and the statement there that the Father is greater than the Son.

---

[125] Gregory *Third Theological Oration* XIV.

[126] Somewhat intriguingly for the present debate, the Cappadocian insistence on the primacy of the Father has made some question whether there is not a latent Arianising subordinationism in their theology, despite themselves.

Obviously this verse had proved something of a happy hunting ground for Arians. However, the Cappadocians tend to deal with this in a nuanced way. The following statement from Basil catches it well.

> I believe that even from this passage the consubstantiality of the Son with the Father is set forth. For I know that comparisons may properly be made between things which are of the same nature. We speak of angel as greater than angel, of man as juster than man, of bird as fleeter than bird. If then comparisons are made between things of the same species, and the Father by comparison is said to be greater than the Son, then the Son is of the same substance as the Father.[127]

What is striking in this line of argument is that Basil recognises that degrees of greatness can apply between things of the same nature. It is true that as an alternative he suggests that we could read the verse as referring to Jesus the Son in the humility of his Incarnation, but what is vital for our purposes is that he does not rule out of court the idea that one member of the same nature can be greater than another member of the same nature. Comparison in which one is greater is possible without that becoming an inferiority of nature. This casts doubt on the idea that he accepts the Arian proposition that obedience necessarily entails ontological inferiority on the part of the one who obeys. As it happens Gregory makes the same point when he writes of John 14:28:

> ...and the evident solution is that the Greater refers to origination, while the Equal belongs to the Nature; and this we acknowledge with much good will. [128]

Gregory's reference to 'origination' here is to be taken as a reference to the personal relationship of eternal begetting and being begotten that subsists between the Father and the Son. Equality, however, is something that Gregory attaches to the category of nature. It is, of course, standard Nicene theology to accept there are things one says at the level of nature (one substance) while one says something else at the level of persons (three persons). To this extent, Gregory seems to attach equality to the issue of nature and not to the issue of relations between the divine Persons. This, of course, is completely consistent with the argument that eternal subordination properly understood is at the level of relations between the Persons and does not deny equality at the level of nature.

---

[127] Basil Letter VIII *To the Caesareans* 5.
[128] Gregory *Fourth Theological Oration* VII.

4.6.2   Augustine

We must turn now to Augustine both because of his intrinsic importance given his stature in western theology and because he faced Arianism in its later phases, when its arguments had been developed and honed.

4.6.2.1   What Augustine faced

In particular Augustine was looking at a species of Arianism that argued hard on the basis of the differences between Father and Son. Broadly put, one useful Arian argument for the period after 410 A.D. ran along these lines:

a)   All attributes that God has are essential to him. (In other words God cannot be who he is without the attribute in question).

b)   The Father has some attributes that the Son does not (for example, the Father has the attribute of not being begotten, the Son has the attribute of being begotten).

c)   All the Father's attributes are essential to him.

d)   So the Son does not have essential attributes of God, namely the attributes that the Father alone has (in particular, being unbegotten).

In its way, this is quite impressive.

A variation on this is to turn it round so that we talk about attributes that the Son has that the Father does not, such as, especially, being begotten. Since the Father does not have this attribute (he is unbegotten), but the Son does and since we know the Father truly is God, it follows that Jesus the Son has some non-divine attributes, and therefore, conclude the later Arians, cannot be God.

This latter version of the Arian argument about attributes can also make use of ideas about eternal subordination in this way: if one says that the Son is eternally subordinate then he has an attribute (being eternally subordinate) that the Father does not, and consequently, since this must be a non-divine attribute, the Son cannot be God. On this version the stress on eternal subordination is not just that the subordination itself shows the Son is a lesser being in terms of nature, but also since this is not shared with the Father, this shows that it cannot be a divine attribute and therefore its possessor cannot be God since some of that attributes that person has are not divine.

We should note something very striking at this stage. The relational asymmetry between the Father, the Son and the Spirit is precisely what opens Nicene theology up to this kind of late Arian argument based on essential attributes. For it is the relational asymmetry that means there are real relational differences between the Persons of the Trinity. If the Trinity were to consist of 'three friends', who were relationally symmetrical to each other and who were not relationally different from each other, then such a Trinity would be far less open to this range of Arian argument. The disadvantages, of course, would be leaving behind the biblical revelation and losing the personal unique distinctiveness between the Persons.

4.6.2.2   Augustine's answers

Augustine develops a range of answers to the arguments of late Arianism that he faces after about 410. A critical framework for this is the way he tackles the Arian thrust about all divine attributes being essential. Augustine makes two key moves here. First, he observes that some attributes are relational, that is, one is something by virtue of a relationship with someone else. This kind of argument about co-relativity had been used before by Athanasius and Origen. Within the category of co-relative relationship there can be difference and asymmetry: a father is not a son in his relationship with his son, and he is to that extent different, but he is a father only by virtue of that relationship. He is a father because he has a son, some-one else distinct from him who stands in that relationship to him. Similarly a son has his position or place in the relationship between him and his father. He is son within that relationship and his father is not, but he only is son because there is some-one else distinct from him who stands as father to him: there is asymmetry within these co-relative relationships.

However, Augustine combines this idea of relational attribute with something else. He asks, in effect, what the argument about essential attribute is trying to protect theologically. It protects the vital thought that God does not change and that each and all of his attributes are 'unlosable'.[129] We should add that one of the reasons why change and losability matter so much is that if God does change then he may change from being loving and merciful and may exercise his will so as not keep his promises of salvation. If his promises are not seen as wholly reliable, we may withdraw our faith. Yet if the relationship itself is eternal and unchanging, then the relational attribute of, say, being father, cannot be lost. It is an eternal and unchanging attribute of the

---

[129] The language of unlosability is drawn from *De Civitate Dei* XI.10. See too *De Trinitate* VI.8.

Father, yet one he enjoys by virtue of relationship with his Son, not one he shares with his Son. Other attributes which are not relational in this way but relate to the substance or nature of the Father (goodness, wisdom) can indeed be seen as 'essential' in the conventional way.

This means that by these two moves, Augustine is able to draw a distinction between attributes of relationship and attributes of nature/substance. Since he is dealing with eternal relationships, he can quite happily admit the Arian point that nothing non-essential can be posited of God.[130] Indeed, Augustine insists on it. However, the use of eternal relational attributes enables him to account for the differences between Father and Son.

This framework fits perfectly well with what we have seen in Athanasius and Hilary. For both of them, sons obey in their relationship and this is on a different level from the equality of nature that sonship also entails.

That said, within this framework Augustine produces several different answers to the late Arian challenge. Thus with regard to John 6:38, Augustine explains how our security in the hands of the Son rests on the way that the Son has come to do his Father's will.[131] This is then developed in terms of humility and Augustine's distinctive sense that pride is the root of all human sin.[132] The Son teaches humility by his doing of the will of the Father, and is the teacher and 'master' (*magister*) of humility.[133] Augustine comments: 'Whereas pride doeth its own will, humility doeth the will of God.'[134] Augustine contrasts fallen human pride with the humility of the Son and adds a very striking phrase:

> Thou wouldst perhaps be ashamed to imitate a lowly man; at any rate, imitate the lowly God (*Puderet te fortasse imitari humilem hominem, saltem imitare humilem Deum*).[135]

Augustine therefore links the doing of the Father's will very firmly with the Son's humility in taking human nature and the earthly life that the Son then leads. To this extent one could wonder whether this is simply an example of the Son's obedience in the human nature, as the

---

[130] *De Trinitate* V.3.
[131] *Tractate on John* XXV. 15.
[132] He also sees it as central to the sin of the fallen angels.
[133] *Tractate on John* XXV. 16.
[134] *Tractate on John* XXV. 16.
[135] *Tractate on John* XXV. 16.

arguments of Giles and others would suggest. Yet there is also his striking phrase 'the lowly God' (humilem Deum). This raises the interesting and hugely significant question of whether the Son is humble in eternity before his Father as a distinctive relational attribute. Put sharply, the question becomes 'Was the Son humble before the Incarnation?' This matters because it relates to whether humility is a virtue found in the Trinity in eternity. This in turn affects our views of power and goodness. However, this needs to be resolved by a closer look at the texts in John since Augustine does not develop the matter at length here.

It is also clear that Augustine would indeed be hostile to some ways of putting the subordination of the Son. Thus he is unhappy with what he sees as a crude idea of the Father 'giving orders' to the Son to create.[136] Apart from anything else, what words would the Father use to give orders when the Son is himself the perfect Word of the Father? No doubt part of the reason for this antipathy is the introduction of a disjunction between Father and Son, and in particular the introduction of a time gap and temporal succession into the relation between Father and Son. This emerges explicitly when considering the temporal aspect of the 'word of command' (1 Thessalonians 4:15).[137] Given the way Augustine wants to stress the unchanging 'unlosability' of the relational attributes, these are very logical concerns. Indeed they strongly resemble the concerns of Basil.

Nevertheless, as we have seen, Augustine rejects key premises of the Arian project. He does not think obedience necessarily means inferiority of being. He writes:

> But however much God the Son obeys God the Father, is the nature of a human father and human son different, because the son obeys the father? It is something utterly intolerable on your part that you want to prove from the obedience of the Son a difference of nature between the Father and the Son. Moreover, it is one question whether the Father and the Son have one and the same substance; it is another question whether the Son obeys the Father.[138]

Augustine makes two points here. First, in the case of human sons, we do not say obedience proves an inferiority of nature. Secondly, he clearly

---

[136] *Answer to the Arian Sermon* III.4.
[137] *Answer to the Arian Sermon* XIII.
[138] *Answer to Maximinus the Arian* II, XVIII, 3.

distinguishes between the two questions of, on the one hand, 'one substance' (and therefore equality of nature) and on the other hand the obedience of the Son to the Father. It is clear that he leaves open precisely the option that one may have the obedience of the Son without compromising his equality of nature.

Having drawn this distinction, he goes on:

> Hence, if true reasoning admits that the equal Son obeys his equal Father, we do not deny the obedience, but if you want to believe that he is inferior in nature by reason of this obedience, we forbid it. [139]

It is singularly unfortunate that Giles, while citing from Augustine with apparent freedom, does not deal with this aspect of Augustine's argument in the Maximinus debates, but regrettably he does not advert to the debates with Maximinus in any significant way at all, even though these are later writings and deal with some of Arianism's more sophisticated presentations.

4.6.2.3 Augustine's concerns

Overall, we note in Augustine a real concern to preserve the biblical data, notably the asymmetry of relations between the Persons. Augustine is insistent that the Trinity is not a community of three friends, but a trinity of Father, Son and Spirit. Within this framework of relational asymmetry, he wants to preserve the Father as 'beginning' (principium), and it is hard to miss the parallels with the Cappadocian insistence on the Father as Cause (Aitia). Clearly, though, Augustine will want any account of subordination to be couched at the level of relationship and Person, not substance/nature and will also insist that it must not introduce change or succession into the relations. He also introduces very strikingly into the discussion the question of the Son's humility, and whether we are to see this solely in respect of his nature or whether it is part of his eternal relationship with his Father. The phrase 'humble God' (humilem Deum) is very suggestive here.[140]

With this in mind, though, we must examine whether Athanasius and Hilary, who clearly do see the relations between Father and Son as having an obedience element, had any biblical warrant for arguing for eternal subordination. We turn now to perhaps the central biblical source text for Trinitarian theology, John's Gospel.

---

[139] *Answer to Maximinus the Arian* II, XVIII, 3.
[140] *Tractate on John* XXV. 16.

5 John's Gospel

5.1 Introduction

At first blush it might seem over-ambitious to refer to John's Gospel for a defence of the Son's eternal subordination. After all, Giles quotes the eminent C.K. Barrett to this effect in support of his own position:

> '...[John] more than any other writer in the New Testament lays the foundation for a doctrine of a co-equal Trinity"[1]

Perhaps, however, those wanting to defend the eternal subordination of the Son need not be too disheartened by this citation of Barrett by Giles. For, on the page immediately preceding the one Giles cites, Barrett says this:

> John emphasizes both the humanity of Jesus ... and his inferiority to the Father (5:19; 7:16; 10:29; 14:28). The latter passages are not to be simply explained away as having reference only to the humanity or incarnate life of our Lord. The eternal Son (not the incarnate Jesus merely) was sent by the Father (3:17 and often), to speak the Father's words (14:10; 17:8) and to perform the Father's works (14:10).[2]

In other words, far from supporting Giles' argument, Barrett explicitly disagrees with it. This, however, is far from evident from Giles' citation. In fact, Barrett sees no inconsistency between a full-blooded affirmation of the Son as equally divine with the Father and speaking about the Son's 'inferiority'. Equally, Giles does not advert to Barrett's assertion that the relevant passages cannot be 'explained away'[3] by restricting their ambit to the incarnation. Indeed, puzzlingly, he shows no awareness of Barrett's statement at this point.

We begin substantive consideration in this section with three observations, two from Hilary of Poitiers and one from Karl Rahner.

First of all Hilary insists that God is his own best witness and we must exercise care not to measure what he is or can be according to the

---

[1] Giles, *The Trinity and Subordinationism* p 34 fn 4, quoting C K Barrett, *The Gospel According to John* (London: SPCK, 1962) p 78.

[2] Barrett *The Gospel According to John* p 77.

[3] Barrett's striking phrase *The Gospel According to John* p 77.

limits of our own rationality.[4] This means that as far as possible we must allow God to disclose not only that the Trinitarian relations are those of Father, Son and Spirit,[5] but what kind of sonship, fatherhood and spirithood are involved.

Secondly, Hilary emphasises that both Arianism and Sabellianism have a common aspect to their heresy: they both deny the true sonship of the Son. The former do this by insisting he is a creature rather than a son; and the latter do this by insisting that he is the same person as his Father, and therefore not true son.[6] Both of these heresies make these assertions on the basis of the need to defend monotheism and the divine monarchy. It is, we must say again, easy to forget today how central the issue of monotheism is.[7]

Thirdly, Rahner famously remarked that the economic Trinity, that is, the Trinity revealed to us in salvation history is the immanent Trinity, that is, the Trinity as it exists in eternity, and vice versa.[8] The precise extent of this dictum has been much discussed but its fundamental thrust has been widely applauded. Minimally Rahner underlines that there is continuity between the economic and immanent Trinities:[9] the immanent Trinity does not, so to speak, contradict itself in the way the economic Trinity works. This in turn means minimally that the economic Trinity reveals the immanent Trinity. Rahner's point, like Hilary's, warns us against speculating what the Trinity 'must' be like or 'could' be like. Instead we must focus on the data of revelation and the events of the Incarnation in particular.

5.2   Summary of material from John

John's Gospel amongst other things deals with the distinctively Trinitarian revelation of God: of God who is the Father of the Son, of

---

4   *De Trinitate* I.18.

5   As opposed, say, to Creator, Redeemer and Sustainer. Trinitarian theology is not just a question of asserting Threeness, but the kind of Threeness disclosed in the Bible.

6   *De Trinitate* I.16 and 17 – Hilary describes both as leaving a solitary God in eternity.

7   Although monotheism remains a key issue in relations with Islam and Judaism, as well as our assessment of Jehovah's Witnesses and Christadelphians.

8   Rahner, K. *The Trinity*, Donceel, J. trans. (London/New York: Burns and Oates. 1970) p 22.

9   In particular writers such as C M La Cugna suggest that the economic Trinity 'exhausts' the immanent Trinity: there is no immanent Trinity outside the economic. The question asked of this view by some is whether this ultimately erodes the distinction between creator and created.

Jesus who is God incarnate and the Son of the Father, and of God the Spirit sent by the Father at his Son's behest. In this Trinitarian revelation the personal, relational identity of Father and Son is central and their identities are co-relative (each is who he is by virtue of the relationship with the other) and asymmetrical.

In this asymmetrical and co-relative relationship, there is deep but asymmetrical love between the Father and the Son. The Father's love is paternal in that he loves his Son and accordingly, as a father, is lavishly generous both in eternity and within time: in eternity he gives the Son the same kind of life that he has himself, life-in-himself (uncreated life); and within the framework of created space and time he gives his Son all things in creation as his to rule over. The Son's love is filial in that he loves the Father and reveals this by his obedience to his Father and his will.

This all means that the Father's primacy of will is contoured by his other-personed love of the Son and the Son's love is shown in his obedience. To remove the Son's obedience is to remove the revelation of his love. Further, to remove the Son's obedience eliminates the way by which Jesus himself refutes the charge that his claim to deity undoes monotheism. Thus eliminating the Son's filial obedience would be disastrous within John's theological framework.

5.3   John – The centrality of sonship

R Bultmann famously quipped that John is a Gospel about the Revealer, but the Revealer reveals only that he is the Revealer. This has a grain of truth in that Jesus in John's Gospel is the focal point of his own revelation. However, Jesus reveals specifically that he is the Son of the Father, and consequently can both reveal God and save humanity.[10] His identity as Son is therefore critical to the Gospel's project, an obvious but important point to make.[11]

Not only does Jesus reveal that he is Son, but this is, clearly, a contested revelation. Of course Jesus' revelation is contested in several dimensions in the Gospels (whether he is compromised by associations with drunkards, whether his criticism of the Pharisees etc. is true,

---

[10]   He also reveals the true state of the 'world': John 7:7.

[11]   The soteriology of both Athanasius and Hilary requires the full deity of the Son: in Athanasius only the creator can redeem (see *De Incarnatione*), and in Hilary only the infinite God can meet the problems of human finitude and sin (*De Trinitate* I). On either formulation, if the Son is not fully God, he cannot save.

whether he is demonic etc.), but a critical dimension of opposition in John's Gospel is whether by claiming to be God's Son he has committed blasphemy by making himself equal to God – making himself a second God. This way of putting Jesus' 'blasphemy' emerges most clearly at John 5:18 and 10:33 and is implied in 8:58-9 and 19:7.

John chapter 5 is fundamental here, because it discloses the primary dynamic the Gospel gives for the rejection of Jesus by those to whom he is sent – his claim to be the Son. Up until chapter 5, in chapters 1-4, opposition to Jesus has been muted, although, after the Prologue, clearly anticipated.[12] But as Jesus makes explicit his claim to be the Son of God, determined opposition to him focuses on the issue of sonship. In particular, what the objections have in view is whether Jesus' claim to be son is a blasphemous breach of the principles of monotheism. In this way chapter 5 sets out the frame of reference within which the mounting rejection of Jesus in the following chapters takes place. Vitally, John's corporate character 'the Jews', when asked by Pilate, finally crystallise their objection to Jesus on the issue of Jesus' claim to be 'the Son of God.' Since chapter 5 is so significant in the discussion about Johannine sonship, the decision of Giles 2002 to have only some 7 dispersed references to John 5:17-30 seems, again, odd. One needs a concentrated look at this section of John 5 if we are to grasp what Jesus means by claiming to be son.

This means that a critical theological question set by the Gospel is how Jesus can be son without being a second God, that is, a rival who breaches the injunction to monotheism set out in Deuteronomy 6:4. Monotheism is a fundamental issue John's text sets before us, as the patristic theologians rightly saw. Their focus on this question is well-taken because the Trinitarian debate in John focuses so strongly on it: we might say the Gospel's Trinitarian theology is framed from this perspective of 'rival second God'. Does Jesus connect himself as Son to his Father so as not to be a 'second god' through an egalitarian relationship, subordination or in some other way?

This point must be stressed: the text of John itself foregrounds the question of how Jesus as 'son' is not polytheistic. This in turn means that part of the way we must weigh the competing theologies of egalitarian and subordinate Trinitarian thought is by whether they answer this issue at all, but further, much more importantly, whether they answer it in the way that John does.

---

[12]   See John 1:10ff.

5.4   *Sonship is asymmetrical*

In fact while the relationship between Father and Son in John is enormously close, it is asymmetrical: in relational terms, as distinct from questions of substance, the Father and Son are different persons, with unique attributes within their relationship.[13] They are inseparable and co-relative: they are, after all, in an eternal relationship, but in John this is a relationship where each is who he is by virtue of relation with the other. But that relationship is emphatically that of father and son. Augustine notes and insists on the point that they are revealed as father and son, not as friend and friend.[14] Augustine's point is telling. Two friends may be two individuals but each stands in the same relationship to the other: each is the other's friend. But a father and son do not just stand as individuals in relationship to each other: they are individuated within their relationship: one stands as father to the other, but not as son, and the other stands as son but not as father. Each is who he is by virtue of the relationship, but each is individuated and not simply a mirror image of the other. They are asymmetrical in the relationship. This asymmetry is particularly clear with regard to two major Johannine motifs:

- The motif of sending, in which the Father sends and the Son is sent;

- The motif of giving, in which the Father gives to the Son and the Son receives.

We bear these motifs in mind as we look in some detail at John 5:19-30 where both sending and giving motifs are present.

5.4.1   *John 5:19-30*

5.4.1.1   *Context*

John 5 is self-contained, set between two Jerusalem geographical markers (4:54 and 6:1), with the action taking place in the theologically significant arena of Judaea/Jerusalem (5:1).[15] It is also replete with forensic elements (law-breaking; blasphemy; testimony; witness; judge and accuser).[16]

---

[13]   The closeness of the relationship is shown by, amongst other things, the mutual indwelling language.

[14]   See especially the critical section *De Trinitate* VII.7.

[15]   Significant because of the association of Judaea/Jerusalem with rejection and death for Jesus.

[16]   See J Neyrey *An Ideology of Revolt* (Philadelphia: Fortress Press, 1988) p 11, Witherington *John's Wisdom – a Commentary on the Fourth Gospel* (Westminster: John Knox Press, 1995) p 136 and Harvey *Jesus on Trial – A study in the Fourth Gospel* (London: SPCK, 1976) p 50.

5.4.1.2   Structure

We can see three movements:

- a sabbath healing which leads to **accusation** of Sabbath breach (vv 1-16),

- a **defence** to this initial charge of Sabbath breach. The defence strictly starts in v 17, but then broadens to deal with a further charge, this time of blasphemy related to monotheism and proceeds to v 30,

- a **testimony** section from verse 31 onwards where Jesus 'calls' different testimonies which validate his claim and culminates in the accusation of his accusers because they will not listen to the testimony Jesus has (notably in 5:45).

We focus here on the middle, defence section. This focus is appropriate because in it Jesus is answering the charge that he is establishing himself as a second god, thereby breaching monotheism. Following J. Neyrey's analysis,[17] the defence has two stages. Jesus is accused first of breaching the Sabbath (v 16). His first defence to this initial charge is in v 17, in which he claims to be doing what his Father is doing. This turns on the vital principle that 'his Father' can do such things on the Sabbath lawfully.

This principle recalls the tradition that God exercises the prerogative powers of deity, judgment and the giving of life, on the Sabbath. The creator king of the universe does not stop being that on the Sabbath.[18] God does not breach the Sabbath by being creator king and life-giver on the Sabbath. We need to relate this to the question of the divine monarchy. God exercises his divine monarchy on the Sabbath, shown by the lawful exercise of his prerogative sovereign powers. To exercise those powers is a **monarchical** act. The monarch can rightfully do such acts. For another to do those monarchical acts independently and without his permission would be implicit treason. It is implicit treason because doing the monarchical acts is a tacit claim to be the monarch. In the same way, if someone sits on a monarch's throne, it is a tacit claim to be the monarch. If these monarchical acts are done by virtue of another free-standing independent rule, then the monarchy has been breached.

Jesus' defence in v 17 to the charge of Sabbath breach is therefore that he is innocent because he is entitled to exercise the prerogative

---

17   Following Neyrey *Ideology of Revolt.*
18   Again following Neyrey *Ideology of Revolt.*

powers of deity on the Sabbath and does so as God's Son. If God his Father can lawfully do these things on the Sabbath, so can he. Unsurprisingly, this provokes an extreme reaction. Since it is a monarchical act to exercise the prerogative powers, Jesus' claims to exercise those powers necessarily raise the question of whether Jesus has breached monotheism by infringing the cosmic monarchy and exercising a free-standing, independent monarchy or rule of his own. Divine monarchy and monotheism are precisely the agenda questions these verses set.

Hence Jesus' words lead to a new and different accusation which is even more serious than Sabbath breach: Jesus is making himself 'equal to God'. This is an almost inevitable development. After all, it looks as though he is proclaiming himself as another God alongside God, a rival king because he claims to have the same prerogatives.[19] How could he have those same prerogative powers without being a rival cosmic king?

This means that a different issue from Sabbath breach is now in view. The issue now at stake is: how can Jesus be a Son with the prerogative powers of God without a breach of divine monarchy and monotheism in its Deuteronomy 6:4 form?[20] Has he set himself up as a rival king in heaven?[21] This means that a further defence is now needed because there is now this new charge. This new charge underlies the rest of the chapter (and indeed recurs throughout the Gospel) but in the immediate context leads us to the second stage of Jesus' defence set out in vv 19-30, his defence against this second charge in which he must explain how as Son he is not a second rival God. To this we turn.

5.4.1.3   *The substance of Jesus' second defence vv 19-30 – the asymmetrical Father-Son relationship*

Jesus has to show how he is not a second rival cosmic lord. He does this by co-ordinating his judgment and life-giving with that of his Father: their actions are *integrated*. **Their actions are not the competing actions of rivals.** This means that the divine monarchy of the cosmos continues

---

[19]   Modalist Monarchianism would answer that, of course, by asserting that the Father and the Son are the same person.

[20]   We must recall that many pantheons spoke of gods who were fathers and others who were sons and who were fully polytheistic. Why should the use of father/son language not be equally polytheistic?

[21]   After all, in Greek mythology, sons do displace their fathers as 'king of the Gods': Kronos replaces his father Ouranos and is himself displaced by his son Zeus: see Hesiod's *Theogony*.

to be one rule. Jesus explains his Sonship in terms both of what his Father has given him and also what his Father has sent him to do. In other words, his explanation is in terms of subordination, and not in terms of role egalitarianism. Subordination is a key part of his defence of the divine monarchy. This emerges in the following way.

First of all, there is the literary structure of Jesus' defence. Verses 19a-30 form an *inclusio*, beginning (v 19a) and ending (v 30) with the theme that Jesus can do nothing by himself.[22] In the context he is renouncing action that is independent of his Father. The way that v 19a and v 30 top and tail this adds emphasis to the point that they are making. Those verses stress Jesus is not acting separately from his Father as, so to speak, an alternative cosmic king.[23] His actions are integrated with his Father. But vitally, he is not just saying that he acts in concert with another, it is not just that it is a question of joint action decided on as between two friends. Rather, the repetition between v 19a and v 30 underlines how this integration is achieved. The integration turns on Jesus the Son doing the will of him who sent him (verse 30). Jesus is not an independent operator, but one who has been sent by another, and, if that other has a will that Jesus does, then that other has a will which is distinguishable from Jesus' and which Jesus performs.[24]

The intervening verses, vv 19b-29, further explain this integration or co-ordination between the Son and his Father. This integration is explained in terms of the Father's love for his Son, his will in sending Jesus and his giving to Jesus.

Thus in his love for his Son, the Father has shown his Son his works (v 20) and wants his Son to be honoured as he is honoured (v 23). The balanced comparison between the honour given the Father and the honour he desires to be given to his Son clearly suggest that Jesus is to be given equal honour with the Father, that is, divine honours. This is reinforced both by the stated purpose of verse 23 (The Father has given the prerogative powers to this end) and also by what naturally follows from having the prerogative divine powers: we worship God because, amongst other things,

---

[22] From v 31 the argument moves to what evidence supports the case that Jesus has made in vv 19-30. The topic from v 31 is broadly that of witness.

[23] There can be no theomachy, or battle between the gods, as in, for example Hesiod's *Theogony*, or divergence of purpose between different deities as, say, between Apollo and Athena who want different sides to win in the Trojan war.

[24] Which tells against modalism, as Tertullian rightly stressed and is also problematic for Gregory of Nazianzen's construal of the Gethsemane prayer as reflecting one single numerical will for the Father and the Son.

hc has the powers of life and judgment. By his healing on the Sabbath, Jesus has already demonstrated that he has precisely these divine prerogatives. Further, the Father has given Jesus the same kind of life ('life in himself') as he himself has (v 26). In all this, the Father's will is carried out by the one he has sent, who does not act independently but instead implements the will of him who sent him (vv 19 and 30).

Jesus' deity is fully affirmed by several features here. He has possession of the divine prerogatives (giving life and exercising judgment) by the Father's will.[25] The will of the Father in giving the prerogative powers is that his Son should have the same honour as he, the Father, does himself. The emphasis is not on what Jesus wants, nor on his 'seeking after' equality with his Father.[26] Rather the point is that it is the Father's will, as distinct from the Son's, that is in issue. Jesus is not a 'bad' son like Absalom or Adonijah who are rivals to their father. Further, given the OT prohibition on worshipping anything or anyone but God, this will of God the Father is itself decisive. The jealous God is not a jealous Father when it comes to the honouring of his Son. This is vital for preserving the divine monarchy: the exercise of the prerogative powers (and hence the exercise of the monarchy) is done by the Son because the Father wills it. The Father is other-personed in wanting his Son to have the same honour as he does. The Son is therefore not independent, but traces his rule back to the will of the Father. In exercising sovereignty towards creation, he obeys his Father.

Related to this, but also significantly different, is the way the Son possesses 'life in himself', or uncreated life, by the gift of the Father.[27] We note here once again the motif of the Father giving to the Son. This provides continuity with the other instances of the Father's giving mentioned in this section.

However, what is given here, 'life in himself', in particular precludes an understanding of the Son as a creature.[28] Two aspects are

---

[25] And is therefore innocent of the charge of breaching the Sabbath: he is fully divine and can give life.

[26] There is a lurking contrast with Adam and Eve in Genesis 3 here.

[27] Note here both the absolute terms of God's revelation as 'I am' in Exodus 3:14 and the way God differentiates himself from idols precisely on the basis that they are created and he is uncreated: see Jeremiah 10:1ff, especially vv10-11: God is the uncreated creator of all, while idols are the created non-creators. Jeremiah 10:10 is hugely important here for its assertion that God is the true God.

[28] As Hilary rightly saw. For him John 5:26 was a keystone in refuting the Arian case precisely because the Son and the Father have the same kind of life. See *De Trinitate* II.11.

in view here as we analyse 5:26. First, there is the comparison between the life the Father has and the life given to the Son. This strict comparison emerges from the verse because there is structurally a parallel introduced by the terms 'just as... so'. But also the strictness of the comparison is then reinforced by the repeated phrase 'life in himself'. This means that if we are to understand the kind of life that the Son has, we must look at the kind of life the Father has.

The Father, of course, is the uncreated creator: the kind of life he has is sharply different from creatures, precisely because he is not created.[29] This introduces very starkly the idea that since the Son has life in himself just like the Father, he has 'uncreated life'. Creatures are indeed given life, but this is not life which is the same kind of life as their creator, life-in-himself. The obvious difference between our 'life' as creatures and the life God has is that our life remains radically contingent and dependent. It has a beginning. We cannot say we have 'life in ourselves'.[30]

However, the principle of integration between the divine actions of the Son and the Father is not that both simply consent to the Son doing certain actions as symmetrical partners. Instead there is a consistent asymmetry.

The Father is depicted as the one who sends Jesus and who gives, not so much here to us, but rather Jesus stresses in this passage what the Father gives to his Son: divine prerogatives, uncreated life and equal honour. This is, we must stress again, profoundly other-personed. Moreover, it is completely unenvious, because the Father wants the Son to be honoured in the same way that he is. Given the OT emphasis on God's holy jealousy for his honour, this is remarkable.

The Son therefore is depicted as one perfectly integrated into his Father's will and purpose, as part of that purpose and certainly as its beneficiary, but distinguished by his submission to his Father's will. That is why he is not a second God.

Thus if we were to ask Jesus what gives him the right to judge, his answer refers us back not to an intrinsic authority that is his and his

---

[29] Climactic OT statements about monotheism in Jeremiah 10:1ff and Isaiah 40-55 contrast God with idols on the basis that God is the uncreated creator while idols are created/made non-creators. This is what marks him as 'true God' (note especially Jeremiah 10:10 here).

[30] Hilary closely connected the 'life in himself' of John 5:26 with the self-existent life of Exodus 3:14 and 'I am'.

alone, something that essentially does not need the Father. But neither is it that this is an agreement he and the Father have reached. His answer is that his Father has given him this right, which in turn implies he is cosmic judge **derivatively**, because this is his Father's will which is exercised in love towards him. To receive authority in this way is to acknowledge that it is the giver's to give in the first place.

The risk therefore of asserting a simple role egalitarianism is that this suggests another basis for the cosmic judgment that Jesus is entitled to exercise than the one he himself accepts and uses to justify the point that he is not a second rival god. Role egalitarianism tends to suggest not so much the asymmetrical giving of a father to a son, but rather a taking as of right as between equal friends, which does not depend on the generous giving of the other. But after all, Jesus cites his Father's gift and will as the basis for his judgment, not that he is his Father's equal in role.

5.4.1.4   Alternatives to subordination?

At this point we must turn to the contention of Giles and others that any obedience is in Jesus' human nature only. This is unwarranted. Vitally, if vv 19-30 only refer to the Son in his humanity then the basic charge lodged against Jesus in v 18 remains unanswered. Jesus has claimed divine prerogatives in terms of his eternal relationship as Son to the Father and the issue is how **in eternity** he is not a second God, in contravention of Deuteronomy 6:4. The question of why Jesus is entitled to exercise the prerogative powers of cosmic divine monarchy is not confined to the Incarnation. The issue is how that cosmic divine monarchy can be intact if Jesus is 'son' at all, irrespective of the Incarnation. The Arian argument is looking at the Father-Son relationship outside the Incarnation and why it threatens monotheism and the divine monarchy. The Arian argument is not restricted to the relationship between Father and Son within the Incarnation and in the Son's human nature. Giles' approach eliminates an answer based on Jesus exercising divine monarchy in obedience to the Father's will. Instead the egalitarian answer provides a solution which is not that which Jesus himself gives and which leaves unanswered the charge Jesus faces of breaching the principle of monotheism.

In fact, the context of vv 19-30 shows Jesus is answering the charge of v 18, and for his answer to work, it has to apply outside as well as inside the Incarnation. Moreover, to answer the monotheism problem by appealing to role egalitarianism takes us well beyond what is revealed here – precisely the kind of speculative theology that Hilary and Rahner warn against, as Tertullian did before them. Jesus does not explicitly speak in role egalitarian terms at all – quite the contrary.

Given that role egalitarianism is not explicit here, one next asks whether it emerges by good and necessary consequence. But it does not: the idea that the Son receives gifts in obedience from the Father not only emerges clearly from the text but provides an eminently coherent answer to the point at issue – namely how Jesus as son does not undermine monotheism and divine monarchy. Instead the emphasis on the will of the Father and the notes of obedience suggest that such implications would be contrary to the context and not required by it.

We may also conveniently at this point turn to Moltmann's contention that 'abba' language is intimate but precludes authority.[31] In fact the Gospels record the word 'abba' only once on Jesus' lips in Mark 14:36. This is during his Gethsemane prayer when he asks for the removal of the 'cup' but concludes 'not what I want but what you want' (NRSV). Tertullian notes in his arguments against modalism that Jesus' prayers must be taken as prayers by the Son to his Father understanding them as two distinguishable persons.[32] As such, Jesus the Son is praying precisely on the basis that he and his Father have distinguishable wills and that – very explicitly – he submits to his Father's.[33] It is impossible to see how this explicit language of submission becomes teaching which supports the plainly opposite idea of non-submission. Moltmann's case therefore fails.

With these considerations on John 5:19-30 in place we turn more generally to the central thematic issues of sending, giving and love in John.

5.4.2   Sonship and sending

5.4.2.1   The Son, as sent agent/shaliach

P Borgen's seminal work on agency in John emphasised the way Jesus is consistently presented as one sent by his Father into the world and

---

[31] See Moltmann *The Trinity and the Kingdom of God* p 69 n 17; p 70 n 19.
[32] See *Against Praxeas* 23 – if there are not two persons when Jesus prays, Tertullian argues God would be a liar/deceiver (*mendacem*).
[33] Moltmann cites J Jeremias on the use of 'abba', but, as others have noted, e.g. M M Thompson, Moltmann also glosses out that Jeremias himself saw 'abba' as intimacy **with** authority. Jeremias actually says: 'He spoke to God as a child to its father: confidently and securely, and yet at the same time reverently and **obediently**. [emphasis added]': see Thompson 2000 *The Promise of the Father: Jesus and God in the New Testament* (Louisville: Westminster John Knox Press); p27 from J Jeremias (2012) The *Prayers of Jesus* (London: SCM), pp 62-63.

who acts in his name.[34] In particular, Borgen pointed to the way that in Jewish halakhic understandings the agent is seen as fully representing the principal, the one who sent him.[35] He *is* his principal, one might say. This resonates with the way that treatment of Jesus is indicative of treatment of the Father – rejection of the Son counts as rejection of the Father (John 5:23), and acceptance of the Son as who he is is not merely an acceptance of the Son but also constitutes acceptance of the Father and his truthfulness (John 3:33). But there is still asymmetry between principal and agent, for, as Borgen notes, as between the agent and principal, the agent is appointed by the principal and is subordinate or obedient.[36] Jesus takes up just this line of thought in John 13:16 where he puts master and 'the one who sends' in parallel. This parallelism does not suggest an ontological superiority (for those who send may be as human as those who are sent, masters are as human as those who serve them). It does, though, strongly suggest that 'master' and 'he who sends' are in corresponding positions of authority. 'Master' and 'sender' are connected by the way Jesus puts them in parallel. To this extent, the fact that the Son is sent readily suggests he is obedient, and as sender, the Father's authority is suggested.

5.4.2.2   The Son as unique agent/shaliach

However, as Borgen also pointed out, there is something unique about the way that Jesus is portrayed as agent/*shaliach* of his Father. He seems able to be an agent in a way that other prophets cannot (although other prophets may also be described in one sense as 'sent by God' – in particular John the Baptist is a man sent by God (John 1:6)). In part this uniqueness is underlined by the consistent way that Jesus speaks as coming from or being sent from above and not being 'of' this world (see especially John 8:23). He is sent from 'outside', which does not seem to be true of ordinary prophets. Moreover, because he is sent from 'outside' he is privy to knowledge about God that does not arise from within the world (e.g. John 3:32) and this is tied to who he is personally as Son. It is as Son that he is sent from above in the way he is. This sending therefore has unique dimensions.

An agent/*shaliach* is not necessarily a son, but this one is, and his personal identity, as Borgen hints, is intimately connected to his

---

[34]   P Borgen 'God's Agent in the Fourth Gospel' pp 137-148 in J Neusner (ed.) *Religions in Antiquity* (Leiden: Brill, 1970).

[35]   Borgen 'God's Agent' p 138f.

[36]   Borgen 'God's Agent' p 140.

function as agent/*shaliach* sent into the world. Only God's Son could be this kind of agent/*shaliach*. Put another way, to be the kind of agent/*shaliach*, sent into the world, as he claims, Jesus' Sonship is divine sonship, with an ontological dimension to it, not just the sonship of common will and purpose.

5.4.2.3   *Agent/shaliach and asymmetry*

There remains, though, this asymmetry about sending as agent/*shaliach*. The consistent usage in John is that the Father sends the Son, and not vice versa. The use of the individual personal names of 'Father' and 'Son' suggest that the sending cannot just be taken as 'the triune God generically' sending the Son. Rather the sending is in the context of the personal relationship between the individual persons of Father and Son. Since that relationship of Father and Son is eternal, this sending is not reducible simply to the human nature. And sending has something irreducibly asymmetrical about it: someone sends, and someone else is sent.

5.4.2.4   *The use of 'sending' in the Arian controversy*

This notion of sending became a bone of contention during the Arian controversy. Late homoian Arianism (e.g. of the kind Augustine encountered in the period 415-425 in North Africa) argued that the sending of the Son by the Father showed that the Son was obedient and therefore he was also ontologically inferior to the Father. After all, they said, to be sent implies a relationship of obedience and to be sent into the world from outside cannot be just an obedience during the Incarnation because the sending into the world 'starts' before the Incarnation.

The pro-Nicene response was varied, but it was not simply along the lines Giles and others would advocate. They did not simply respond by saying that the Son's obedience was confined to the Incarnation, although they were perfectly familiar with this kind of argument and used it elsewhere. Apart from anything else this would not explain the language of 'sending' the Spirit. Obviously that cannot be explained by reference to action in a human nature. Rather than the Giles argument, a very frequent point was that sons obey fathers and we do not say of a human son who obeys his father because of his relationship as a son that he is a lesser being ontologically than his father.[37]

5.4.2.5   Sending and the doing of the Father's will

We have noticed Borgen's point that in general in agency the agent is obedient to his principal.[38] How true is this of the sending usages in the Gospel?

We have already seen that John 5:30 has Jesus saying that he does the will of the one who sent him. The significant thing here is the way that the two themes of 'sending' and 'doing the Father's will' are put together. This explicit collocation of doing the Father's will and being sent by him occurs elsewhere. Thus, in 4:34 Jesus says that his 'food' is to do the will of him who sent him. Again in 6:38 Jesus says that he has come down from heaven to do the will of him who sent him. In this latter case we should also note the presence of a third motif along with 'will' and 'sending', that of coming down from heaven. We have already seen how Athanasius interprets this of the relationship of Father and Son outside the Incarnation as well as within it.

Similar ideas of doing the Father's will but without using that precise phrasing also occur. In John 3:34 it is declared that he whom God has sent utters the words of God, thereby aligning his teaching with the one who has sent him.[39] In a similar vein in 7:18 Jesus legitimates his teaching as not being his own, but the teaching of the one who sent him. As in his defence speech of 5:19ff, Jesus resists the suggestion that he has independent standing which could rival his Father by co-ordinating his teaching with that of his Father. And this co-ordination is not simply saying 'we agree' but that the teaching is the Father's in the first instance: it is 'his'. John 8:26 picks up the theme that Jesus teaches what has been given to him by his Father and this is reinforced in 14:24.[40]

---

[37] Thus Augustine comments in his confrontation with homoian Arianism: 'Of what else are they trying to convince us by these testimonies of the sacred scriptures but that the Father and the Son have different natures, because the Son is shown to be obedient to the Father? They would not of course, say this in the case of human beings. After all, if a human son is obedient to his human father, it does not follow that the two of them have different natures.' See *Answer to Arian Sermon* VI.6. See too *Answer to Maximinus* II.xiv.8 and 9. Augustine has other interpretative strategies to answer Maximinus but this is the best.

[38] Borgen 'God's Agent' p 140.

[39] It is not entirely clear whether the speech of John the Baptist which begins in 3:27 continues through vv 31-36.

[40] In John 17:8, believing that Jesus is sent by the Father is joined to the reception by the disciples of the words that the Father gave Jesus to speak.

Especially important in this regard is 12:49, where Jesus re-asserts that he does not speak on his own authority but has been given a 'command' about what to say and what to speak. This brings to a head the idea that what Jesus reveals in his words is what his Father has given as a command to say. Jesus explicitly says, therefore, that what he reveals is a matter of obedience to the one who sent him. This is not an obedience to 'God' generically, but to his Father, the one who sent him. The relations between the Trinitarian Persons are here in view.

Naturally, we must return here to the argument of Giles and others to the effect that the Son only obeys as a human being. This argument has to deal with the way that the **mode** in which the immanent Trinity reveals the Trinity's relations, which involves the Son obeying the Father who sent him, actually stands at odds with the **content** of that revelation, namely that the Son is not in a relation of eternal obedience to his Father who sent him.

This requires some comment. Naturally, we must observe that the refutation of Monarchian modalism by Tertullian and others was predicated precisely on the point that the **mode** of revelation of God (there are apparently two distinct persons in the economic trinity, shown for example in the prayer of one to the other) did not mislead about the **content** of revelation about the immanent trinity (the Monarchian modalists were wrong to say that the apparent two persons of the economic trinity actually revealed only one person).

This, though, is not a complete refutation of the Giles argument. For it might be said that the mode of revelation is that of embodied speech conveyed by a physical medium and Christian orthodoxy holds that the immanent Trinity is incorporeal and hence does not utter speech in that way. The embodied speech of Jesus in the Incarnation does not show that the Trinity is corporeal. In the same way, it might be argued the obedience of Jesus in the Incarnation does not have to show a relation of eternal obedience. Further, upholders of the Giles line might argue that the Son only 'does the will' (i.e. obeys) once he has been sent, that is, once he has been incarnated.

However, as observed above, the pro-Nicene refutations of Arianism from Athanasius and Hilary do not use the arguments Giles suggests. The reason, of course, is that the Arian arguments they faced were rather more searching and sophisticated than some might think today. Certainly the Giles argument meets Arian objections which are framed with respect to the earthly ministry of Jesus (subject to what we must say about John 14:31 and the love of the Son for the Father below). However, Arian arguments about the obedience of the Son were not confined to the earthly ministry of Jesus. They argued that the Bible tells us about the obedience of the Son outside the Incarnation, citing, amongst other things, Genesis 19:24. They also cited the language of 'sending' in John's Gospel, not simply with a view to the Son's obedient actions *after* he arrived in the world, but rather also taking 'being sent' as *in itself* an obedient action: the Son was not merely obedient once he had taken human flesh, but was obedient in the very taking of that flesh. The Son is himself humble in his true deity even in the taking of human flesh (compare Philippians 2:6ff) so too he is obedient in being sent. Notably the Arians might cite here John 13:16 where Jesus comments that a servant is not greater than his master, nor a messenger than the one who sent him. The very fact that the messenger is sent suggests obedience, especially when put in parallel with the case of servant and master.

In the face of these objections, as we have seen, Athanasius and Hilary (and at points in his later work Augustine) do not contest that 'sending' is only in respect of Jesus' human nature and thus restricted to it. Rather their answers concede that sending does involve filial obedience and they make a positive use out of this because they use to argue that the Son is a true son and not a rival second god. 'Sending' is part of their strategy of integrating the actions and life of the Father who sends and the Son who is sent in such a way that monotheism and divine monarchy are preserved. Since the Son is sent by the Father, he is no rival to the Father. They make, so to speak, a virtue out of the sending precisely so that the Father and Son can be integrated as one God at the level of eternity. They have to do that, because that is where the Arian attack is being mounted.

Further, there is a hostage to fortune in saying that 'sending' with its obedience implications does not apply to the Son in his deity. If we were to say that then this risks applying to the humility of the Son as well, as evidenced by Philippians 2:6ff. For if the obedience in being sent does not apply to the Son in his deity, why should his assumption of humanity be seen as humility by the Son in his deity?

At first blush this may not sound very serious. In fact, though, it raises the question of the moral perfection of the Son in his deity. Traditional accounts of the perfection of God suggest that God is not merely the source of physical existence for his creation, but the source of every moral virtue in it as well.[41] In the language of classical theism,

---

41 See e.g. Anselm *Monologion* 1.

God does not merely have a virtue (as a human being may have the virtue of justice) but God *is* that virtue infinitely and perfectly so that it is held by him totally – he *is* justice, because every aspect of justice is realised in him perfectly.

Now, on the Giles argument and indeed that of Moltmann, one inevitably starts to wonder whether the triune God is perfect in this way. The virtues of obedience and humility seem to have no place within the immanent Trinity because when they are revealed in the Son, the Giles argument seems to locate them exclusively in his humanity. It seems, then, that humans have virtues that the triune God does not. We return to this question later.

That said, some might still ask whether the sending/*shaliach* motif takes us unquestionably to the life of the Trinity in eternity and outside space and time and should not rather be seen as linked to the human nature in the Incarnation. This would be despite the use of sending with respect to the Spirit. But while there is force in the observation that the Son becomes incarnate in Mary's womb because there has already been a sending by the Father, is there something still more unambiguous about the contours of this asymmetrical relationship in eternity?

For this, we turn to the motif of giving in John's Gospel.

5.4.3   The giving motif

5.4.3.1   Giving in general

We should begin with the obvious observation that giving also involves an asymmetry. There is a donor and donee. Frequently 'gift' also has an association of something unearned and thus readily says something about the character of the donor and his/her relationship with the donee. Gifts are readily associated with generous affection and love on the part of the donor. For the donee, the response very readily is (depending on the gift) gratitude. In this asymmetry between donor and donee, love can be involved on both sides but in an asymmetrical way: the donor loves in giving generously; the donee loves in appropriate grateful response.

In assessing how generous and loving a donor is, and what kind of response is apt from a donee, the nature of the gift is important.

5.4.3.2   Giving in John

These considerations matter as we consider giving in John. As one looks at John one realises that giving is a consistent motif. Perhaps our first instinct is to look to the rightly-loved statement about divine generosity in John 3:16, in which we are told that God loved the world and gave his Son. However, this focuses us on a very particular giving: it is a giving in time and it is a giving to us. As such, it deals with giving within creation. One has to ask whether divine giving is simply something that takes place within and is restricted to creation because it features creatures as donees. It is certainly wonderful that God does give to his creatures, but one has to ask what it is in God's eternal character that eternally roots this temporal giving which takes place within the framework of creation.

In fact, key passages in John about giving take us to the giving specifically of the Father, not so much to us, but to his Son, and this giving to the Son takes place both in time and space, but also in eternity. Other givings emerge in John, notably giving to believers,[42] but giving between Father and Son is in effect where this pattern starts.

We have noted already that the Father gives the prerogative divine powers to his Son (5:19-30). In a sense the giving of divine powers of rule could be said to relate primarily to a giving within creation or co-extensive with creation. But even more strikingly the Father has given 'life in himself' to his Son. This giving cannot be said to be within or co-extensive with creation because the 'life-in-himself' that the Father has and which he gives to his Son is uncreated life. This giving of 'life in himself' in John 5:26 therefore is eternal in nature rather than limited to the economic life of the Trinity in salvation history. We should add that the Father has given works for the Son to do to the Son (e.g. 5:36) and words to say (12:49; 17:8; 17:14) but in particular has given believers to the Son (e.g. 6:39f; 10:29) and indeed has given 'all things' (3:35; 13:3; 17:2; 17:7). Notably in the case of the giving of all things this is based on the love of the Father for his Son (3:35). This, then, is what the Father is like with his Son: he loves him and shows that by bestowing gifts on him – vast gifts.

Thus it is, naturally, good to dwell on the Father's love for the world (3:16) – but this must not obscure the deep love of the Father for his Son.

This means that 'giving' is a profoundly significant theme in John for our understanding of the Father. This giving motif characterises the Father as profoundly and prolifically generous: what more could he give his Son than 'life in himself' and authority over all things? What more could he give to believers than his Son? But the giving motif also covers

---

[42] Especially the Son, the Spirit, life and faith are given to believers.

both time and eternity and does not allow us to see a gap between economic and immanent trinities. Thus we clearly find giving in eternity (the giving of 'life in himself' [5:26] is by definition in eternity) and in space and time (e.g. the giving of believers [6:39f]). Giving is also an asymmetrical motif, and depends on the donor having the right or sovereignty to make the donation. Jesus grounds his authority not by appeal to his ontological equality with the Father, but on the grounds of what his Father has given him and his conformity to his Father's will in the exercise of that authority.

This takes us to a final theme in John, the love between Father and Son.

5.4.4   *Love between Father and Son*

We rightly stress, following Richard of St Victor, that the Trinity is a community of Persons who are full of other-personed love towards each other, not a 'private love' of oneself.[43] However, Richard also stressed that each of the loves each Person had towards the others was unique and individuated because they were each unique individuals standing in their distinctive relational positions. He was right to do so, because while John's Gospel tells us about the asymmetry of the Persons as Father, Son and Spirit, it also tells us something of the unique, individuated nature of that love. Richard rightly saw that this nexus of shared, uniquely individuated loves related to the perfection of God,[44] and we may also say that it vitally concerns us since this goes to the fundamental identity of the triune God with whom we are now in relationship as adopted children of the Father. Indeed it is not merely that we are in relation to each Person of the Trinity and therefore deeply involved in whether their fundamental characters are loving or not, but we are also *instances* of the intra-Trinitarian love in the sense that the Father has given us to the Son in his love *of his Son* and the Son receives and holds us in his love *of his Father* who gives. We are not given by the Father to the Son simply and solely because the Father loves *us*, although it is true he does. The giving of believers by the Father to the Son takes place within the network of intra-Trinitarian loves. The contours of intra-Trinitarian love are of exceptional significance to us.

---

[43] 'For nothing is better than charity; nothing is more perfect than charity. However, no-one is properly said to have charity on the basis of his own private love of himself. And so it is necessary for love to be directed toward another for it to be charity.' *Trinity* 3.2.

[44] Richard's argument in *Trinity* 3 is that the perfection of God indeed **demands** this kind of love.

5.4.4.1   The love of the Father for the Son

We have already stressed the love of the Father for the Son revealed in his giving to his Son – within creation, he has given all things and in eternity he has given 'life in himself'. What we do well to underline at this point is the Father's generous wish that his Son be honoured as he is.[45] This is a genuine and striking instance of looking to the benefit of another, even when it means 'sharing' glory with another. There are strong qualities of humility and lack of envy on the part of the Father here in his relationship with his Son. We will return later to the significance of the humility involved in the Father's love for his Son.

5.4.4.2   The love of the Son for the Father

What is not always appreciated is that Jesus tells us about his love not just for us but for his Father. We should, of course, expect that a perfect son will love his father. But Jesus explicitly states his love for his Father in John 14:31. As several commentators note, this is the only time in the New Testament that Jesus explicitly speaks of his love for his Father.[46] It is therefore of considerable significance. However, it matters still more widely because of the theological significance of whether the Trinity is a 'community' in which love is mutual and reciprocal between the Persons as against a community where love is only from the Father towards the other Persons. We do well, therefore, to spend a little time examining this unique statement of the Son's love for his Father.

The passage comes towards the end of the first major division of the Upper Room Discourse.[47] The comment 'Rise, let us be on our way' (14:31) forms a punctuation before Jesus resumes his instruction with the simile of the true vine (15:1ff). For R Brown, 14:31 comes very near the end of a section in chapter 14 where Jesus concludes this first major division of the Upper Room Discourse with a section bracketed by remarks about being still with the disciples (14:25) and needing to go (14:31).[48] However, the themes in this concluding section of departure, love, obedience, the Spirit and the ruler of this world all occur elsewhere in chapters 13-17 and chapter 14 in particular.

The sub-section 14:30-31 is variously translated. The NRSV reads:

---

45   Hilary catches the significance of this for the Arian debate well: 'It is only things of the same nature that are equal in honour.' *De Trinitate* IX.23.
46   E.g. R E Brown (1971) *The Gospel according to John* II p 656, J Ramsey Michaels (2010) *The Gospel of John* p 797.
47   Following the kind of division suggested by Brown (1971) *John* II p 581ff.
48   Brown (1971) *John* II p 649.

(30) I will no longer talk much with you, for the ruler of this world is coming. He has no power over me; (31) but I do as the Father has commanded me, so that the world may know that I love the Father. Rise. Let us be on our way.

The NIV puts it slightly differently:

(30) I will not speak with you much longer, for the prince of this world is coming. He has no hold on me, (31) but the world must learn that I love the Father and that I do exactly what my Father has commanded me. Come now; let us leave.

These translations deal with an original order of the different clauses in the Greek NT that goes like this:-

a)   but that the world may know that I love the Father

b)   and/even as the Father commanded me

c)   so I do

d)   Rise, let us go from here

These differences in translation reflect in part different decisions about punctuation and whether to take the clause at the beginning of v 31 ('so that the world may know that I love the Father') with what precedes it in v 30 (the NIV's position) or with what follows (the NRSV's position). A further difference is that the NIV sees the clause at the beginning of v 31 as expressing obligation ('the world must learn') as against the NRSV's construal that this is a purpose clause ('so that the world may know').

On balance it is preferable to take the opening clause of v 31 as a purpose clause,[49] and as introducing a fresh thought, given the introduction of that clause by a strong 'but'.[50] Even so, it is a mistake to

---

[49]   The ἵνα construction of v 31a more obviously refers to purpose or result than to establishing a necessity. The syntax is certainly compressed in this verse, since it is not immediately clear what the main clause or thought is that introduces the ἵνα clause. The two main possibilities are that the last clause of verse 30 introduce it, or that the clause is proleptic and in fact depends on what follows in the rest of verse 31 and anticipates what will produce the purpose or result in question.   D A Carson (1991) *The Gospel according to John* p 510 notes either is possible. Commentators who do attach the clause to the end of verse 30 nevertheless reach broadly the same conclusions on the connection of love and obedience. This is no doubt because the word 'and' (καὶ) which introduces the second clause of verse 31 is readily taken as epexegetical, that is explaining what immediately precedes it. This means on any of the main punctuation views the second clause of verse 31 shapes our understanding of Jesus' love for the Father.

[50]   See J Ramsey Michaels (2010) *The Gospel of John* pp 796-7.

over-state the differences that flow from these varying construals: when the 'must' in question is a divine 'must' there are clearly strong elements of purpose and likewise a divine purpose readily carries obligations and necessity. It is not unfair, then, to see the opening clause of v 31 as indicating that there is a purpose and obligation that the world knows that the Son loves the Father. Jesus and the Father want the world to know this.

What is more this purpose or desire is in conjunction with a sequence ((b) and (c) in the framework set out above) constructed as a parallel about obedience on the part of the Son.[51] Broadly the parallel is (in somewhat literal terms):

- as the Father commanded me

- so I do

This parallel creates a sense of precise match between what the Father commands and what Jesus does. The NIV's 'exactly what' is an apt equivalent for this. The thought, of course, is not new, since just this match between what Jesus does and what the Father wills or commands has been a key theme by which divine monarchy/monotheism has been affirmed from chapter 5 onwards.[52]

However, a significant question here is how closely the affirmation of Jesus doing just what the Father commands (his obedience) is tied to the purpose about demonstrating or revealing the Son's love for his Father. In a sense this is yet another presentation of the major issue concerning the eternal subordination of the Son as to whether love and obedience go together. So far we have seen Jesus (as recorded in John) meet objections based on the need to preserve monotheism and the divine monarchy by reference to doing the will of his Father. Now the question is not just whether there is the presence of love from the Father to the Son in this monarchy (John 5:19ff shows that there is such paternal love), but whether the doing of the Father's will in this monarchy also reflects and reveals the love of the Son for his Father.

Certainly commentators do tie the revelation of Jesus' love for his Father very closely to his obedience. Carson's comment is representative:

The world may think, with the devil, that Jesus is defeated by his death. It must learn that Jesus is vindicated in his death, and that the

---

cross, resurrection, and exaltation of Jesus Christ ultimately turn on the commitment of the Son to love and obey his heavenly Father at all costs. The love relationships within the Trinity (to use a term that developed later) are logically prior to the love of God for the world.[53]

Two important observations flow from this. First, Jesus' saving acts towards believers are not on this view primarily inspired by Jesus' love for sinners. It is true he certainly does love sinners, but the 'logical priority' on which that love rests is that of the Son for his Father, as Carson rightly notes. Secondly, the implication of speaking of this 'logical priority' for the love relationships within the Trinity is that these relations are eternal: the eternal love of the Son for his Father is revealed by his obedience within space and time.

In terms of syntax, some commentators take the parallel '... and as the Father commanded me, so I do...' as an immediately following explanation or teasing out of the revelation of the Son's love for his Father.[54] There certainly is an acute proximity within the verse, but this junction of the Son's love with his obedience is not just created by the verse itself, but becomes more intelligible when the love/obedience theme of the preceding and succeeding material is borne in mind.

Again, commentators rightly note that earlier in chapter 14 the love of believers for Jesus is manifested by their obedience to him (see 14:15, 21, 23, 24).[55] We are, further, given a parallel between the Jesus:believer relationship and the Father:Son relationship in 15:9 (compare also 17:18). The formula is, so to speak, along these lines: as the Father to Jesus, so Jesus to his believers. Given this parallel relationship, it is not surprising to find both believers and Jesus manifest their love for Jesus and the Father respectively through the same attitude, namely their obedience. What is more, lack of love on the part of a believer is manifested by lack of obedience (14:24).

This all means that there is a recurrent theme of the connection that one can show love for another in certain relationships by obeying them.

---

[53] D A Carson (1991) *Gospel* p 509. Carson's comment is all the more telling since he is following the NIV's translation and punctuation of 14:30-31: Carson (1991) *Gospel* p 510.

[54] E.g. Brown (1971) *Gospel* II p 656: 'What this love consists in is made clear by the second line [sc. the parallel phrase], for the "and" that joins the second line to the first [sc. the purpose clause] is epexegetical ... the love consists in doing what the Father has commanded, just as the Christian's love for Jesus consists in doing what Jesus has commanded.' See also H Ridderbos (1997) *Gospel* p 513. The point here is how the 'and' at the start of the parallel clause functions.

[55] Obedience by the believer is associated with abiding in Jesus' love in 15:10.

Naturally, the recurrent nature of this theme suggests that John 14:31 is not a verse out on its own. It may be true that the explicit statement of the Son's love for the Father occurs only here, but once we see how all the other indications in John's Gospel of doing his Father's will are to be read in terms of love for his Father, then we can see that the Gospel is replete with the love of the Son for the Father as well as emphatic about the love of the Father for the Son. This connection of love and obedience is extraordinarily significant for a world that sees obedience as showing anything but love, either on the part of the one who obeys, or the one to whom obedience is given. If we ask whether Jesus loves his Father, he points us precisely to his obedience as revealing just that. His love for his Father is evidenced here on earth by his obedience.

This may be counter-intuitive in our culture which tends to envisage love and obedience as mutually exclusive categories, but unmistakeably Jesus puts obedience as revealing love, both obedience by himself with regard to the Father and obedience by his followers with regard to him. We note further that this sits at odds with Moltmann's idea that there is no obedience between Father and Son. It also sits extremely poorly with the Giles thesis that obedience is only with regard to Jesus' human nature. Strikingly Giles *The Trinity and Subordinationism* has no indexed reference to John 14:31 even though the revelation of the Son's love for the Father cries out for comment because of its intrinsic theological significance.

We need, though, to ask whether the Giles line of argument nevertheless provides a good fit for John 14:31. The first issue is obviously whether there is anything in the text of John 14:31 that explicitly leads us to see this as an obedience confined to Jesus' human nature. The answer here is 'No, there is nothing explicit to that effect.' The next question is whether a limitation of the obedience to Jesus' human nature arises by good and necessary consequence. Again, the answer is 'Nothing necessarily leads to that reading'. For while it is true that the obedience in question does seem to have the earthly ministry of Jesus in view, this is in the context of the relationship between the Father and the Son and this is obviously not confined simply to Jesus' human nature.

But if the Giles reading is neither explicitly present nor demanded by good and necessary consequence, are there other good theological reasons for wanting to take it? This takes us to the significant matter of the way the Son reveals the Father and his relationship with the Father. If Giles and others were right, and that the relations between Father and Son only featured obedience in the human nature, then it obviously follows that the Son's obedience does not tell us about the Son's love in the eternal relationship. This, though, drives a wedge with regard to the Son's love between economic and immanent trinities, between the triune God as revealed in space and time and as he is in eternity. After all, the economy shows the Son's obedience and this obedience shows the Son's love for his Father, but according to Giles and others this is not what the immanent trinity is like.

Aside from the fear that this falls into conforming God into what we think he 'must' be like in our western cultural image, this opens up a still more serious problem. If the Son's obedience does not reveal the contours of his love in eternity for his Father, what does reveal that love? Why would we think the Son loves the Father? In a similar vein, we might ask what the Father's love for the Son is like if it is not in having a purpose in which the Son obeys and fulfils the Father's will for the Son's glorification?

The Giles line of argument attenuates what is revealed to us of love between the Persons of the immanent Trinity through the economic Trinity. This, though, is not how Jesus appears to envisage revelation taking place. Thus Philip asks to see the Father (14:8) and in the context this is asking to see God as he really is, not exhaustively perhaps, but certainly truly. Jesus' response in 14:9-11 underlines the reality of the revelation that exists currently (if one has seen Jesus one has seen the Father) and also that the Father has been identified with the works Jesus has done. This is explained in terms of the way that the Father and Jesus the Son mutually indwell each other – something that occurs during the Incarnation as well as outside it. This all tends to join economic and immanent Trinities closely together so that while the economic Trinity may not exhaust the immanent Trinity, it is nevertheless continuous and consistent with it.[56] The economic Trinity is not at odds with or contradictory to the immanent Trinity. As such the relations of loving filial obedience and loving paternal provision that we see between the Son and Father in the economic Trinity are rightly taken as revealing the relations of the immanent Trinity. At this point one realises that the difficulties over the Giles line of argument relate to how the Son's eternal love for his Father is truly revealed and whether the Father-Son relations of the economic trinity are in conflict with those of the immanent trinity. Ultimately, on Giles' case, the obedience of the Son reveals a non-obedient love. This fatally undermines the Incarnation as genuinely revelatory of the Trinitarian relationships.

---

[56] This is part of the strength of Rahner's contentions about the relation between economic and immanent trinities.

6 Considerations arising from the dyothelite Christological dispute

6.1 Why the Christological question of dyothelitism matters

So far we have been considering the Son's eternal subordination in relation to Trinitarian theology: the charge of Arianism is, after all, characteristically thought of as a Trinitarian heresy. However, we also need to consider alternative ways in which an objection to the Son's eternal subordination might be put. With this in mind, we turn to the area of Christology, the doctrine of Christ, and dyothelitism in particular since this area also deals with the will, or wills, of Christ.[1] Naturally, the issue of the will in Christ is central to the issue of the Son's eternal subordination.

6.1.1 Summary of the argument over the dyothelite controversy

The objection to the Son's eternal subordination might be made that subordination is simply a category error because the Father, Son and Spirit share the same divine natural will, that is will at the level of their common nature (using 'nature' in its technical Trinitarian sense). In fact, this objection does not refute the point that at the level of personal relationship rather than nature, the Son is subordinate to his Father. This is attested in the prayer in Gethsemane, and is entailed by the Son's unity at the level of person, whereby, although he has two natural wills, they are not opposed to each other. Alternative arguments to the effect that the Son does not obey, or only obeys in the Incarnation both fail to deal with the Gethsemane prayer at the exegetical level and risk dividing the personal unity of the Son.

6.1.2 Chalcedon and the dyothelite controversy

A convenient summary of the Chalcedonian Definition of 451 is that Jesus the Son is fully human and fully divine and yet fully one, unified Person. This ruled out various unorthodox positions to the effect that he was not fully and always divine (adoptionism), that he was not fully human (Docetism and Apollinarianism), that he was a composite of deity and humanity but not fully either (Eutychianism) and that he was not a fully unified Person, but divided (Nestorianism).

---

[1] Dyothelitism postulates that there are two wills in Jesus Christ the Son.

The way in which Chalcedon did this was to use the grammar of Nicene theology with its categories of Person and Substance/Nature. This grammar had allowed the pro-Nicene orthodox to explain how the Godhead was many (three at the level of distinguishable but inseparable Persons) and yet one (one indivisible nature which each Person fully is). Chalcedon in effect uses the same framework which distinguishes Person from Substance/Nature to explain how Jesus the Son is many (in terms of nature: fully God and fully human) and one (a single unified Person).

With this Chalcedonian framework in place, obvious questions which then arose for exploration included whether Jesus the Son had two wills or one. After all, if one says that Jesus the Son has everything that makes for a human nature (mind, appetite etc.) and everything that makes for a divine nature (knowledge, understanding etc.), then a point of intersection is over the will: humans are said to have wills, but so is God. But if Jesus the Son has two wills, is he a divided Person? Would saying Jesus has two wills take one back to Nestorianism, which tended to divide the Person of Christ?

The solution eventually adopted, based on the vital arguments of Maximus the Confessor, was to see Jesus the Son as having two wills, one human and one divine.[2] This was required because 'will' at this point is being defined as an attribute of **substance/nature**, not an attribute of **Person.** If one defines 'will' in this way as an attribute of substance/nature, then it follows as the night the day that one must assert two wills, otherwise one or other nature, or both, will lack something that properly belongs to it, namely 'will' defined in this sense. There are two wills in Jesus the Son, a human will, arising, so to speak, in his human nature and a divine will arising in the divine nature.

However, this gives rise to a line of argument about the single divine will that could bear on the eternal subordination of the Son. To this we now turn.

6.2   Possible implications of the dyothelite controversy

6.2.1   Obedience as a wrong category

Dyothelitism stresses that there are two wills for the eternal Son, arising in his two natures. However, if there is only one divine will, then in what sense could the Son be in a relation of eternal subordination and

---

2   Although final settlement was not reached until the Third Council of Constantinople 680.

obedience to his Father? Surely, it might be said, since there is only one will, it makes no sense to talk of subordination, because one talks of subordination to another's will. But in this case there is no 'other' will at the divine level: just one. As such, surely one has to say that obedience is simply the wrong category.

One might also say that an egalitarian case where the two Persons are related by agreement rather than obedience is equally open to this objection: agreement presupposes the will of another with which one agrees and here there is no such other will. Hence, it might be said, there is no egalitarian agreement either.

This, though, is an inadequate response since it does not actually refute the point that subordination is simply a category mistake, given that there is only divine will in eternity.

6.2.2   The unity of the person of the Son

However, there are substantial difficulties with this objection to the eternal subordination of the Son. On any view, we need to preserve the unity of the Person of Jesus the Son. In a sense this was common ground in the debates between the Monothelites (arguing for one will) and the Dyothelites, notably Maximus the Confessor. The Monothelites were arguing that a plurality of wills divided the Person of the Son, and therefore led one back to Nestorianism and, in effect, having two persons as well as two natures. Sergius of Constantinople made just this point:

> It seems that, for Sergius, two wills in Christ amount to two wills opposing one another, and since it is impious to admit two wills opposing one another in Christ, we must exclude from him two wills and speak of one will instead.[3]

Maximus however argued that simply having a plurality of wills at the level of substance/nature did not necessarily divide the Person of the Son. It is important to grasp the nature of Maximus' response to the line of argument that Sergius was putting forward. Maximus is not disputing that it would be impious to see an internal conflict within Christ between his human and his divine will. Such an opposition would indeed be disastrous. Maximus' point, though, is that the existence of two wills did not necessarily mean opposition:

---

[3]   Bathrellos *The Byzantine Christ* p 75. Arguably Pope Honorius held similar views to Sergius. Pope Honorius' condemnation as a monothelite is obviously not without its embarrassment to Roman Catholic views of the papacy after the 1st Vatican Council.

Why not conceive, as Maximus later did, two natural wills in conformity with one another?[4]

In making this point, Maximus was drawing on a number of themes. First, far from denying the unity of the Person of Jesus the Son, this unity was indispensable to his view. For it was precisely the unity of the **Person** of the Son that guaranteed that the two **natural** wills would not be in conflict. One Person cannot ultimately will inconsistently with himself or herself, even if that person has two ways in which 'will' may be exercised.[5] Secondly, Maximus was describing the natural will, that is, will as something that arises in a nature and to that extent we should stress, as many have done, that 'will' here has a technical and to modern ears somewhat unusual meaning. The meaning of the term 'will' for which the dyothelites were contending was that of the faculty 'in virtue of which one is able to will or act'.[6] As such it belongs in the category of the nature of an entity. This stands in distinction from 'will' as 'the actualisation of these faculties in willing or acting, or even the results, the object willed or the work done'.[7] One might say that the latter category relates more to what 'I' do with my 'natural' faculty of will.

It is one thing, therefore, to say there must be one unified actualisation of whatever faculty of will that I have, but that provided there is this one actualisation I can have more than one natural faculty of will. It is another thing to say that for there to be one unified actualisation of will, there can only be one faculty of will, one 'natural' will. Maximus can argue that his affirmation of the former does not entail affirming the latter. Sergius and Honorius affirmed the latter.

Nevertheless, at this stage much clearly turns on whether the distinctions that Maximus draws can be substantiated biblically, or whether they are fundamentally speculative. If Maximus is correct to stress that the Person or hypostasis provides the unifying point by which the different faculties of the two natures operate, and if he is also correct to see a distinction between will at the level of nature and the exercise/actualisation of that faculty at, in effect, the level of Person, then Maximus' theology does have the resources to cope with the

---

4 Bathrellos *The Byzantine Christ* p 75.
5 We sometimes speak of a person being torn between two possibilities, but even a decision to do nothing is a decision that things are so even balanced that one will do nothing.
6 Bathrellos *The Byzantine Christ* p 74.
7 Bathrellos *The Byzantine Christ* p 74.

eternal subordination of the Son. For the eternal subordination involves a distinction of 'wills' between Father and Son at the level of personal relation and not a distinction at the level of nature. After all, the pro-Nicene arguments we have been examining deal with the relationship between the Father and the Son at the level of Persons: it is precisely as son that Hilary suggests the Son has a filial subordination that does not entail ontological inferiority. To test this further, we must turn to one of the central texts (perhaps in some respects the central text) of the Dyothelite controversy, Jesus' prayer in Gethsemane.

6.3   Jesus' prayer in Gethsemane

6.3.1   The text

Jesus' prayer in Gethsemane is recounted by all three Synoptic Gospels, with minor variations between them. The fullest text appears in Matthew 26:39-46:

> 36 Then Jesus went with them to a place called Gethsemane; and he said to his disciples, "Sit here while I go over there and pray." 37 He took with him Peter and the two sons of Zebedee, and began to be grieved and agitated. 38 Then he said to them, "I am deeply grieved, even to death; remain here, and stay awake with me." 39 And going a little farther, he threw himself on the ground and prayed, "My Father, if it is possible, let this cup pass from me; yet not what I want but what you want." 40 Then he came to the disciples and found them sleeping; and he said to Peter, "So, could you not stay awake with me one hour? 41 Stay awake and pray that you may not come into the time of trial; the spirit indeed is willing, but the flesh is weak." 42 Again he went away for the second time and prayed, "My Father, if this cannot pass unless I drink it, your will be done." 43 Again he came and found them sleeping, for their eyes were heavy. 44 So leaving them again, he went away and prayed for the third time, saying the same words. 45 Then he came to the disciples and said to them, "Are you still sleeping and taking your rest? See, the hour is at hand, and the Son of Man is betrayed into the hands of sinners. 46 Get up, let us be going. See, my betrayer is at hand." (NRSV)

Matthew tells us here about three incidents of prayer in Gethsemane by Jesus (vv 39, 42, 44). The setting is Jesus' torment of soul at his coming Passion (v 37) and the Patristic theologians were surely absolutely correct to see this as of decisive theological and spiritual significance. It tells of the reality of Jesus' humanity in his anguish in the face of death, it reveals the intra-Trinitarian relationship at work in the Incarnation and it shapes our understanding of the Passion as divinely willed rather than as successful human opposition to the Lord's Anointed.[8] This in turn gives exceptionally distinctive contours to Christian spirituality as we see the kind of love and sovereignty at work in the Crucifixion and the real humbling which the Son experiences in the Incarnation and Passion. Going further, that helps orientate our understanding of where God is in human suffering.[9]

It seems that each section of prayer is largely to the same effect, with three elements.[10] The first element relates to what is possible. The second, on the basis of what is possible, asks that the Cup may 'pass by'.[11] The third expresses Jesus' preference that notwithstanding what he has just asked, the Father's will is to take precedence over his own. These references to 'will' are expressed using finite verbs in verse 39 and a noun in verse 42. The verb and noun are drawn from the same word-group *thelō*. The noun form in verse 42 is *thelēma*. Verse 44 does not provide us with direct speech, but simply indicates that it was the same prayer.[12]

In Mark 14:32-42 there is again reference to three incidents of prayer by Jesus (vv 35-36, 39, 41), but with direct speech only attached to the first. The second is evidently the same as the first,[13] and the content of the third incident is not specified, but inferentially (especially in view of Matthew's account) is again the same. The same elements are there: in Jesus' torment of soul he confesses that all things are possible for the Father and then asks for the passing by of the Cup and yet, lastly, for his Father's will to be primary. He uses the *thelō* word-group in a finite verbal form.

---

8   Compare Peter's speech at Acts 2:23 where he underlines both the reality of human wickedness in the Crucifixion and yet the overarching plan and sovereignty of God. For the Crucifixion as the archetypal fulfilment of Psalm 2:1ff see Acts 4:24ff.

9   In this respect Moltmann's insistence that as we seek to deal with human suffering we must look to the Cross is well-taken, even though one may differ on quite how the Cross then shapes our understanding of suffering.

10 Although R T France *Matthew* (Leicester: IVP, 1985) p 374 envisages that the second prayer more definitely aligns Jesus' will with the Father's.

11 Best taken as picking up the OT usage of 'cup' as indicating punishment and suffering: cf R H Mounce *Matthew* (Peabody: Hendrickson/Carlisle: Paternoster 1991) p 243 who refers to Psalm 75:8 and Isaiah 51:17.

12 Literally 'the same word'.

13 Again the phrase used is 'the same word'.

Luke's account comes in 22:39-46. He makes explicit reference to only one incident of prayer, and it is in tightly similar terms to Matthew and Mark. Jesus' prayer is prompted by his anguish and has the same three elements: there is a confession that the Father may 'will'/desire something and then, on that basis, that that the Cup pass by, which is followed by the familiar concluding petition that the Father's will be done in preference to Jesus'. In the element asking that the Father's will be done, the term is again from the *thelō* word-group, this time the noun *thelēma*. Luke's account does differ, though, in that where Matthew and Mark speak of what is possible for the Father ('all things are possible'), Luke speaks of what the Father wants/wills/plans, using a different word-group *boulomai*.

This means that the Synoptic Gospels provide consistent but not completely identical accounts with regard both to substance and to terminology. Prompted by anguish, Jesus prays repeatedly the same kind of prayer:

- some kind of reference to what the Father wants/desires/plans/is able to do;

- a petition on that basis that the Cup pass by;

- a concluding, over-riding petition that the Father's will be done in preference to Jesus'.

Over the years, this sequence of prayers has raised enormous difficulties. Some have felt that Jesus shows an unseemly fear in the face of death. Others feel uneasy about what appears to be a difference of mind and opinion between the Father and the Son. While some of the exegetical results this has prompted may seem outlandish, the impulse to safeguard the unity of the Godhead and the divine monarchy is to be respected.

That said we should note three things: first, Tertullian is surely right to stress that the prayers between Father and Son in the Incarnation do speak of a real distinction of Persons. So, exegesis should not take us down a line that obscures that difference of Persons: that is exactly the mistake modalistic Monarchianism made in its attempt to defend divine monarchy.

Secondly, as a related point, not only is there a plurality of Persons here, but in some sense there is a plurality of wills. Quite what that plurality is remains to be explained, but minimally there is a plurality occurring in regard to the Persons in which something relating to the Father is preferred by the Son to something in himself. That, again, must not be obscured in any explanation.

Thirdly, there is an emotional intensity to what the Son experiences here, and that, likewise, must not be obscured. This intensity is in the context of the 'intimate communion' the prayer indicates between the Father and Jesus the Son.[14]

With this in mind, some major possible construals of what Jesus means with his petition that the Father's will be done in priority over his run roughly like this:

- Jesus' reference to his own will is a reference to his own natural human will only;

- Jesus' reference to his Father's will is a reference to the common divine natural will;

- Jesus' reference to wills is to be taken as a reference not to natural wills but to actualisations of will at the level of persons.

We need now to examine these possibilities for their adequacy.

6.3.2   The relevant possibilities

6.3.2.1   Jesus refers only to his natural human will

On this view, Jesus submits in his natural human will to the divine will. This has the attraction of accepting there is a genuine note of obedience here as the Father's will takes priority, and the Cross is accepted by Jesus in submission. Since Jesus' obedience is integral to our salvation, this preservation of obedience is necessary.

However, this is still an incomplete explanation. The obvious question relates to the divine will and its role in Jesus the Son's experience in Gethsemane.[15] There are two possibilities here. The first is that the reference to the Father's will is a reference to the divine natural will, something that all three divine Persons have in common. The second is that the reference to the Father's will refers to something other than the divine natural will and refers to something properly belonging to the Person of the Father.

This construal to the effect that Jesus refers only to his natural human will therefore needs to be supplemented by considering the second and third possibilities listed here.

---

[14]   France *Matthew* p 373.

[15]   Compare the incompleteness of the exegesis offered by Gregory of Nazianzen: see above.

6.3.2.2   Jesus refers to God's natural will generically

On this view, the reference to the Father's will is a reference to the natural will of the Godhead, something common to all three Persons. But this presents two obvious difficulties. First, one naturally asks whether the writers of the Gospels used 'will' language with quite the terminological precision of Maximus and his peers: would they ever have meant 'faculty of will arising in the nature'? Or is this an anachronistic construction? Secondly, the prayer appears to be a communication between Persons, part of their mutual relationship at the level of Persons. Further, and very significantly, the reference to the Father's will uses the specifically Trinitarian term 'Father', not the generic term 'God'. At first blush, then, one would take the reference to the Father's will as being a reference to something specific to the Father. This is especially the case given that the context of prayer by the Son to the Father brings to the fore a clear personal differentiation between the Father and the Son.

Naturally, it might be objected that at times the term 'God' can be a general way of referring to the Father. This is no doubt true. But the present case is different, for it does not follow that just because the general term 'God' can refer to the Father that the Trinitarianly specific term 'Father', which is a term of differentiation from the other Persons, can be a reference to the triune God generically. Certainly one would need strong contextual support to be sure that the term 'Father' was meant to be read not as a Trinitarianly specific term but instead as a generic term for God. Initially, as we have said, the context seems to be against this, precisely because the setting is that of a prayer by the Son to his Father. This prayer is in the framework of personal relationship.

One has to ask, then, whether there is a further compelling theological reason to displace the *prima facie* meaning of 'Father' as referring to the Father specifically by instead construing 'Father' as meaning 'the triune God generically'. We need here to work through some of the consequences of this position. We can start this by substituting the proposed meaning into the relevant text.

Thus the original text reads:-

yet not what I want but what you [singular] want.

And if we construe this as referring to natural will, this becomes in effect:

yet not what I, that is Jesus the Son, want in my natural human will but what 'you', that is the Father, the Spirit and I, in our joint and common natural divine will want.[16]

This way of putting things at their most explicit highlights some very real problems. Perhaps most obvious is that 'you' on this basis actually comes to include the Son himself. 'You' [singular] on this view in fact means 'we [i.e. plural], including me'. This means that a singular second person reference ('you' [singular]) has become not only plural but shifted from second person to first person ('we'). This completely re-orients the prayer from an address by Jesus to some-one other than himself to an address that includes himself, for the Son is praying not only to the Father and the Spirit but also to himself. How serious is this change from 'you' to 'we'?

Certainly, this is not exactly the same point that Tertullian faced. He refuted the idea that when the Son prays to the Father he prays to himself because the Son and the Father are the same person. However, Tertullian's underlying criticism about modalism in this respect was that it destroyed the revelatory aspect of the Incarnation – the Incarnation did not really tell us the truth about God. Put sharply, Tertullian argued it would be deeply misleading in the Gethsemane prayer to say 'you' when what that really meant was 'I'. Yet it is deeply misleading in a very similar way if when Jesus said 'You' [singular] he really meant 'We'. After all, Tertullian and his fellow anti-Monarchians deplored the way in Monarchianism that what was a prayer to another had in fact become a reflexive, self-addressed prayer, and there is a similar change to a reflexive prayer here.

A second substantial difficulty is that on this view, Jesus the Son is praying that his natural human will be subordinated to the divine natural will which he shares with the Father and the Spirit. This is very close to saying that the Son in his natural human will submits to himself (and the Father and the Spirit) in his divine will. This prompts two further questions.

To begin with, if Jesus the Son in some sense submits in his natural human will to himself in his natural divine will, then in what sense is this a genuine submission or obedience? Submission and obedience seems necessarily to involve the will or desire *of another* which one prefers to one's own. One has conformed one's will to the will of another – someone who is not oneself. For that to happen, there must be a will that is not one's own but belongs to another. But it is just the existence of the

---

[16] Again, compare the construal offered by Gregory of Nazianzen.

divine natural will as the will of another that seems impossible to assert if Jesus the Son has the divine natural will, albeit in common with the other Persons of the Trinity. It is obviously his divine will too.

The significance of this is that if the genuine obedience of Jesus the Son is undermined and his submission is not genuine, then questions inevitably arise as to how Jesus can be the righteous man through whom many are justified (Romans 5:19). Jesus would not save by his obedience. He would not be the new Adam, who remained faithfully obedient when the first Adam did not.

However, some might insist that the existence of the two natural wills does leave space for Jesus the Son to obey in his human nature, and in his human nature obeys the natural will of the triune God. The difficulty this presents is manifest, and relates to the arguments that Sergius and Honorius presented. The strong part of their argument is that one must have a unified integrated Person otherwise one is well on the way to Nestorianism. As we have already seen, Maximus did not dispute the need for any account of Jesus' wills to preserve the coherence and integration of his Person. In what sense, if Jesus the Son wills one thing in his natural human will and another in his divine natural will, is there a genuine, unified, integrated Person? This looks like just the kind of contradiction within Jesus between his humanity and deity which rightly exercised Segius and Honorius. Further, if we were to seek to eliminate this contradiction by simply saying his human will is swallowed up in his divine will, then this clearly raises serious questions about whether he retains all of his human nature in its full integrity.

This brings out the significance of the distinction that Maximus draws between 'will' considered as an attribute of nature which is a faculty by which a Person acts, and 'will' as what is actualised and desired in that natural will. It is perfectly possible for an entity both to have two wills in the sense of a faculty of willing which exists in each nature and for that entity still to have a coherent and unified Person. But conflict arises where the one Person is actualising incompatible things for himself in those two different natural faculties of will. At first glance it appears that precisely this happens if the single Person the Son is seeking in one natural will to obey himself in another natural will. He is seeking both to obey and not to obey. This does look like the kind of conflict within the Person of Christ that Sergius and Honorius feared.

To this extent there are some very significant objections to the idea that the two wills at stake in the Gethsemane are the two natural faculties of will, the natural human will and the divine will. It not only means we must re-construe 'Father' as referring to the triune God generically, but perhaps even more significantly it also creates a real rupture in the unified Person of the Son.

This takes us to the possibility that the Gethsemane prayer is not referring to wills as faculties of nature, but rather will in the context of the Personal relations.

6.3.2.3   Jesus refers to will in the context of personal relation

On this view Jesus' prayer is to be taken quite straightforwardly as a prayer to the Father by his Son, which preserves the priority of revelation in the Incarnation, as Tertullian would demand. The Personal names are to be allowed full weight: the Persons in their personal capacity are in view. Further, the reference to what each Person wills is to be taken within the context of **personal relation** rather than of the common **nature/substance**. As such, Jesus the Son in his unified coherent Person is praying for, and in the light of, the priority of his Father's will in their relationship. This construal leaves intact the dyothelite theology advocated by Maximus and adopted at Constantinople III (680). It is perfectly possible for the one unified Person to be able to actualise the same thing as a Person using two different faculties in two different natures. Far from being inconsistent with dyothelite theology, the eternal subordination of the Son fits well and preserves precisely that aspect, namely Jesus the Son as a unified and coherent Person, which is so important if dyothelitism is not to degenerate into Nestorianism.

This takes us to considering what the two major current arguments in Trinitarian theology against the Son's eternal subordination have to contribute with regard to the Gethsemane prayer.

6.3.3   The Gethsemane prayer and the arguments against eternal subordination

6.3.3.1   Moltmann and intimacy without authority

We recall that Moltmann's case was that 'abba' terminology was not only a distinctive Christian address for God in that it showed intimacy but also excluded authority. As is well known, and as observed above, 'Abba' occurs only once on the lips of Jesus in the New Testament and that is in Mark's account of the Gethsemane prayer. It is also evident that 'Abba' is used here precisely in connection with the priority of the Father's will over the Son's. This remains so, even if one restricts the obedience in question to Jesus the Son in his humanity. He still prefers his Father's will even while calling his Father 'abba'.

The Gethsemane prayer, then, holes Moltmann's case below the waterline.

6.3.3.2   *Subordinate only in the human nature*

We move now to the claim of Giles and others that the Son does obey but only obeys in his human nature. How does this map onto the Gethsemane prayer? Once again it is helpful to substitute in the proposed meaning into the text itself.

On this view, clearly, Jesus the Son's statement:

yet not what I want but what you [singular] want.

Becomes when fully spelled out:

yet not what I as a divine Person want in my human nature but what you [singular] want in your divine Person.

We should recall at this point that those arguing for the eternal subordination of the Son do not deny that the Son does obey in his human nature, that is, through the faculty of will he possesses by virtue of possessing human nature. Indeed, the human obedience of Jesus the Son is strongly asserted and we have seen how important this is for the doctrine of salvation.

But we do at this point become aware of a cavernous silence in this version of the case against eternal subordination. This exegesis of the Gethsemane prayer stresses that Jesus is referring to what he wants or wills in his humanity. This is to be submitted to the Father. Yet we are immediately driven to ask where the will/wants of Jesus the Son in his divinity stand in the Gethsemane prayer.

After all, the logic of the egalitarian position is that Jesus the Son in his divinity is not in submission to his Father but in a relation of eternal agreement and consensus between equals. One has to say this agreement or consensus is eternal because anything less than this opens the door to saying the unanimity of the triune God is contingent and in principle at least open to change.[17] Moreover, since the Son remains fully God in the Incarnation, on the egalitarian case, the

---

[17] We sometimes hear the claim from Open Theism that God changes his mind. We need to ask, if this is so, whether the Persons of the Trinity can also change their minds with respect to their various relationships. Clearly that possibility is not open to classic Nicene theology given the anathemata of the 325 Nicene Creed which stress that the Son does not change. If he does not, the clear and necessary implication is that the others do not either, since they are in co-relative relationship with him.

5

relationship of non-obedient agreement continues in full force during the Incarnation. But if there is such an eternal agreement or consensus which operates during the Incarnation, then it follows that at the very moment that the Son is praying that his wants and wills in his humanity be subjected in his obedience to his Father's will, the Son also fully agrees and concurs with the Father's will, yet not as a subordinate but rather as an equal.

This poses once more some very sharp questions about the unified and coherent Person of Jesus the Son. He seems to have wants and wishes in his humanity that stand at odds to the wants and wishes not just of his Father but also of himself in his divinity, given that he is an equal being in full eternal concord of will with his Father. The prayer to the Father at this point simply seems superfluous: Jesus the Son's will in his divinity simply has to prevail over Jesus the Son's will in his humanity. The issue is not simply 'Does Jesus in his humanity obey the Father?' but 'Does Jesus in his humanity obey **himself** in his divinity?'

On this basis, the egalitarian account of Jesus as only obedient in his humanity encounters some very severe difficulties in the context of the Gethsemane prayer. The question of the value of Jesus' apparent relation with his Father as revealed in the Incarnation is again cast in doubt. Moreover, the unity of the Person of Jesus the Son is open to obvious questions. This in turn has consequences for the genuineness of Jesus the Son's obedience in his humanity. And, if Jesus the Son is not genuinely obedient in his humanity, then this significantly undermines the idea that Jesus is the new, or rather true, Adam, who stood where Adam fell.

For these reasons, not only do we conclude that the dyothelite question does not undermine the argument for the eternal subordination of the Son, but rather one of the key texts in that debate raises acute concerns about the conceivably Nestorian direction of the claim that Jesus wills one thing in his humanity and another thing in his deity. The two natures are said in classic Chalcedonian Christology to find their mutual accommodation in the hypostatic union, the unity of the Person who holds both natures.[18] This is distinctly difficult to hold within the egalitarian framework, since the hypostasis or Person itself docs not seem to be unified.

---

[18] Bathrellos *The Byzantine Christ* p 101 observes of Maximus, 'He sought the unity of Christ not on the level of nature but on that of hypostasis.'

7   The impact of Trinitarian theology on power, individualism and virtue

7.1   *Preliminary*

We move now to consider in more depth the theological implications of eternal subordination. The last century has seen a welcome re-emphasis on the Trinity in Christian thought. This has been true in both Protestantism (e.g. Karl Barth) and Roman Catholicism (e.g. Karl Rahner) while Orthodox theologians such as John Zizioulas have simply continued an emphasis that has, perhaps, consistently been present.

It is, though, worth asking what a Trinitarian theology that includes the eternal subordination of the Son has to offer theologically in the circumstances of the later modern cultural west with its very distinctive and somewhat chaotic combinations of burgeoning regulation, and deep suspicion of power and authority, both of which accompany a strong individualist ethos.

7.2   **Summary**

The late modern cultural West is strongly influenced by thoughts which deeply question how power and authority on the one hand can fit with other-personed love on the other. Some influences see other-personed love simply as one way of exercising power, thereby subsuming love into a general account of power relations: love is a way or pursuing one's power interests. Others see other-personed love as essentially inimical to relations of power and authority. This is compounded by an individualism that accepts individuals but does so as entitled consumers who are essentially uniform and interchangeable. This toxic individualism is also paradoxically prone to a toxic social totalisation, in which the individual is subsumed and commodified as one agent of consumption amongst other essentially similar agents of consumption.

Neither Moltmann's authority-free account nor the account that limits the obedience of the Son to the Incarnation offer resources to encounter these processes. The Trinitarian account that sees the Father as eternally loving his Son paternally and the Son as eternally loving his Father as a Son who submits does offer a way of seeing how other-personed love and authority between ontological equals is both possible and holy. In doing so, it helps us see how obedience and humility are

God-like virtues, since humble other-personed love finds its root in the eternal relations of the three Persons.

7.3 Moltmann's misgivings about power

7.3.1 As there is one power in heaven....

One of Moltmann's great strengths is his insistence that what we say of God inevitably affects what we say about human life on earth. He notes this particularly with regard to relations of power. One of his great fears is the mantra (attributed to Genghis Khan) that as there is one power in heaven, so there is one power on earth. Moltmann is quite right to note that this is a remarkably self-serving statement, and prone to justifying all kinds of abuse. It is no surprise that Moltmann frequently refers back to E. Peterson's essay *Monotheism as a Political Problem* (1935) written against the backdrop of the onward progress of political totalitarianism in 1930s Europe.[1] The title of Peterson's essay is telling: to what extent does monotheism contribute to a monolithic political state?[2] This is a real and perceptive question.

Given this, and given Moltmann's own clear agenda of resisting totalitarianism, it is no surprise that Moltmann is insistent that the relation of the Father with the Son is not and must not be one of super-ordination and subordination: how could it be, when the results on earth of working out the consequences of divine monarchy ('one power in heaven') have been so appalling? Rather, Moltmann takes advantage of the principle 'as in heaven above, so on earth beneath' to propose in effect that as the 'kingdom' of God is a kingdom without authority, so structures on earth must be revised to remove elements of conventional 'lordship'. The eternal subordination of the Son obviously subverts this project.

Yet Moltmann's 'kingdom without a lord' means that the 'arrangements' of heaven, far from being available to legitimate totalitarian and monolithic rule on earth (As Genghis Khan and so many others might want) instead become the very basis on which such

---

[1]   E. Petersen (1935) *Der Monotheismus als politisches Problem. Ein Beitrag zur Geschichte der politischen Theologie im Imperium Romanum.* Hegner, Leipzig ET (2011) in *Theological Tractates* (trans M.J. Hollerich) Stanford: Stanford University Press.

[2]   Others have likewise been deeply suspicious of monotheism e.g. R M Schwartz *The Curse of Cain: the Violent Legacy of Monotheism* (Chicago: University of Chicago Press, 1998).

claims to power are inherently **delegitimated**: the authority claim has no basis in the eternal character of God. Rather the reverse.

7.3.2   'Dominion' against 'Tyranny'

Yet the difficulties here in Moltmann's framework are hard to over-state. Most obviously, the patristic theologians were surely right to see divine monarchy as a given. The data of Scripture is simply overwhelming in this regard, not just because of the consistent use of terms like 'Lord', but because of the monarchical acts God is depicted as doing in both judgment (Passover on Egypt, the Exile) but also salvation (the Exodus is a coercive, monarchical act whose professed aim is to bring God's people out of Egypt so that they may serve him – not Pharaoh).[3] Given the prophecies about Christ's return, it is also clear that monarchical acts of judgment and salvation are not confined to the Old Testament.[4] To that extent Moltmann was clearly wrong to see divine monarchy as a foreign Latin import via Lactantius.[5]

Moreover, if God is not divine monarch then the obvious consequence is that he cannot or does not coerce or compel. But if God's actions fall short of compulsion then he can be successfully resisted at least some of the time. But if he can be successfully resisted, then naturally I must ask whether God can in fact save me from all those who would oppress and exploit me. At some point – especially given our observations of the 20th century which so rightly exercise Moltmann – I need someone who can deliver me from 'the foe and the avenger', no matter how powerful that foe and avenger might be. Certainly my salvation must include the forgiveness of my sins, but it also requires a God who is mighty to save me from all who would oppress me.[6] After all, some oppressors are so powerful and so ruthless that we cannot deliver ourselves from them: this was, after all, precisely Israel's experience in Egypt.

---

[3]   It is no accident that so much of the later chapters of Exodus feature worship: the false worship of the Golden Calf and the true worship that relates to the Tabernacle instructions of God. God is fulfilling his stated purpose to Pharaoh of having his people serve him.

[4]   The Second Coming features coercive acts by Christ against those who oppose him.

[5]   Moltmann *History and the Triune God*, Bowden, J. (Trans.) (London: SCM, 1991) p 6. However, *monarchia* is a Greek rather than Latin word, as Tertullian observes in *Against Praxeas*. Further, pseudo-Justin has a work entitled *On the Divine Monarchy*. It therefore seems odd to attribute the introduction of *monarchia* as a concept to the Latin writer Lactantius.

[6]   In a similar vein, the concession by C Pinnock that we may frustrate God is rather chilling since conceivably one of the ways he may be frustrated by humans is that he cannot rescue when he wants to.

Further, Moltmann understates the way that Christian theology in fact does envisage and has envisaged over the ages that it is precisely on the basis of divine monarchy that abusive structures here on earth can be weighed, criticised and if necessary challenged and changed. Thus Athanasius and Hilary both charged the emperor Constantius with tyranny. Over the course of time later theologians articulated an account of tyranny in which the divine monarch God was seen as the delegator of authority in certain relationships – notably in church, state and family.[7] Since these were delegated authorities, they were authorities held on terms stipulated by the delegator. In fact those with delegated authority remained under law.[8] They did not have untrammelled authority and were not absolute monarchs. They could not be so, since their authority was not free-standing and independent but derived from another higher authority. They became 'tyrants' in their respective spheres when they broke the laws on which authority had been delegated to them, ultimately divine law, in the view of Christian theologians. The political philosopher Leo Strauss writes:

> 'Tyranny is essentially rule without laws, or, more precisely, monarchic rule without laws.'[9]

This aptly captures not just classical Greek reflection on the subject,[10] but Christian theology too. Aquinas phrases this idea slightly differently but to the same effect: the tyrant is one who 'oppresses through might (*per potentiam*) instead of ruling by justice.'[11] Here the stress is on the unrestrained use of power. Indeed the mediaeval debate was not whether tyrants in this sense should be removed, but whether one was entitled to use lethal force to do so.[12]

To this extent there is an alternative strand in Christian thought to Moltmann that does not see the divine monarchy as legitimating

---

7   Notably the influential John of Salisbury in his *Policraticus* VIII.17 (completed 1159).

8   *Policraticus* IV.1, VIII.17. Compare C Salutati (d 1406) 'The special quality of the tyrant is that he does not rule according to law' *De Tyranno* I.

9   Strauss, L *On Tyranny* eds. Gourevitch, V and Roth, M (Chicago: University of Chicago Press, 2000) p 69.

10   Strauss *On Tyranny* is a prolonged reflection on Xenophon's 4th century B.C. dialogue *Hiero*. The Hiero of the title is the tyrant of Syracuse and the dialogue is in part an exploration of whether a tyrant can be truly happy.

11   Aquinas *De Regno* 2, 11.

12   John of Salisbury had argued for the propriety of tyrannicide, while the Council of Constance 1415 later adjudicated against it. Arguably the execution of the usurping queen Athaliah in Judah recounted in 2 Kings 11 is biblical precedent for executing the tyrannical ruler who assumes power without 'law'.

tyrannical or terroristic regimes but rather that because precisely all legitimate power springs from delegation from the divine monarch, the divine monarchy is the legal and practical basis for the accountability of power-holders to God. As such, it is imperative to uphold the divine monarchy: it guarantees not only ultimate salvation and also not just the theoretical accountability of those who abuse power and authority tyrannically but the inescapable nature of that accountability. But, as Moltmann rightly saw, difficulties arise in establishing a divine monarchy within creation if this is completely alien to the character and relationships of the triune God in eternity.

A further difficulty is that Moltmann's egalitarian approach takes us – very naturally – to democratic forms of government. It is, though, one thing to say that democratic government is a legitimately possible and very appropriate way of giving effect to the creation of each human being in the image and likeness of God and another thing to say that democratic regimes themselves enjoy total power and have no higher accountability.

This takes us to a very real contemporary problem: how are we to construe the claims to authority that a democratic majority makes? In one sense this issue was articulated with great force by Alexis de Tocqueville with his concept of 'tyranny of the majority'. De Tocqueville's point with regard to the United States of his day was that all the major areas of political sovereignty (legislature, executive and judiciary) were majority-controlled:[13]

> When an individual or a party is wronged in the United States, to whom can he apply for redress? If to public opinion, public opinion constitutes the majority; if to the legislature, it represents the majority and implicitly obeys it; if to the executive power, it is appointed by the majority and serves as a passive tool in its hands. The public force consists of the majority under arms; the jury is the majority invested with the right of hearing judicial cases; and in certain states even the judges are elected by the majority. However iniquitous or absurd the measure of which you complain, you must submit to it as well as you can.[14]

---

[13] Part of de Tocqueville's acuteness lies in seeing that the separation of powers for which Montesquieu argued in *Spirit Of The Laws* book XI could be subverted by a democratic majority which controlled all three branches of civic power: legislature, executive and judiciary.

[14] De Tocqueville *Democracy in America* I.xv.

There is a difficulty here on the Moltmann scheme. On the one hand, a radical version of the 'intimacy without authority' argument suggests that even the majority cannot exercise authority over the individual: that would be inimical to the values of the 'kingdom'. On the other hand, it is enormously difficult not just to fit this within the biblical framework of passages such as Romans 13:1ff, but also to see how it would work in reality in modern societies given the competition between individuals for the same finite goods.

Yet in addition, Moltmann's point about 'as one power in heaven, so on earth' can indeed be invoked by a democratic majority, that is, a *collective* political ruler can speak in these terms every bit as much as it can be uttered by an *individual* ruler – in fact very possibly with far more plausible claims to legitimacy. And further, if there is no sovereign monarchical power in heaven, as Moltmann contends, then what should or could legitimately restrain the majority? It is for this kind of reason that J L Talmon coined the term 'totalitarian democracy'.[15] Talmon's point was that a democratic regime can in fact manifest totalitarian tendencies, shown notably in its treatment of those who dissent from the democratic majority's views. We should return here to Strauss' comments about tyranny – that it is 'monarchic rule without laws'.[16] When, as de Tocqueville describes, legislative, executive and judicial powers are in fact vested in the democratic majority, then there is indeed a 'monarchic' rule, in the sense of a single consolidated regime of power. It is simply that that regime is not vested in a single individual, but in a collectivity. De Tocqueville's celebrated description that there is such a thing as a 'tyranny of the majority' appears very well-chosen.[17] It is a tyranny because there is no law above it. No law is above the majority because all laws can be altered or modified by the majority.

This brings us close to a central theoretical and practical problem in the current public square: how do individual rights relate to the claims of the majority? This is, of course, one especially sharp version of the more general question of how the individual and the collective relate to one another. If individual rights are simply those rights which a current general opinion accepts,[18] then it is not fanciful to say those rights depend

---

15 See Talmon, J L. *The Origins of Totalitarian Democracy* (London: Penguin, 1986).
16 Strauss *On Tyranny* p 69.
17 De Tocqueville also notes certain patterns of behaviour that flow from this, notably what he calls a 'courtier spirit', whereby not just politicians but citizens find it prudent to flatter and conform to the majority.
18 As the preamble to the European Convention on Human Rights seems to indicate.

on the judgment of the majority as it is from time to time.[19] Aquinas' comment that the tyrant is one who oppresses through power very aptly focuses us on the extent of the power that a majority may claim to have.[20]

Yet the obvious question then becomes this: How we can anchor individual claims against the collective majority without having a rule or monarchy to which the majority themselves are subject? But if we are to say this is a divine monarchy, we also need to ask how this divine monarchy which is exercised with respect to creation is rooted in God's eternal character and Trinitarian relations – his character outside creation, so to speak. To this extent we may well ask Moltmann whether the things that rightly concern him – the avoidance of human totalitarian rule – are not best secured precisely by accepting that there is a divine monarchy, to which all human power-holders are inescapably accountable.[21]

It is important to note that we must talk precisely about a divine monarchy or single rule here. If we were to posit transcendental laws outside the human realm to which humans were accountable but to hold this was polycratic (many independent centres of power), then the obvious question is how those different transcendent but polycratic centres of power relate to each other. There are two basic possibilities here: either those transcendent laws do relate to each other in an ordered way or they do not.

But if they are genuinely independent of each other, then we simply have moral anarchy or chaos on a cosmic scale. This is exactly the point Gregory of Nazianzen makes in his criticism of polyarchic conceptions of the cosmos.[22] The vice of this is that an action can be right according to one centre of authority but wrong according to another. An example occurs with Orestes' dilemma following the murder of his father Agamemnon by his mother Clytemnestra. According to one set of deities, he must avenge his father, but according to another he must continue to honour his mother, no matter what. Is Orestes to be held to account for his killing of Clytemnestra? It depends – whatever he does is wrong or right, depending on which set of deities one listens to. For this reason the

---

[19] It is no answer to refer to the way some constitutions entrench rights as needing super-majorities before being amended. The point is that the majority can amend them. Arguably, it is just when there is a vast majority against my point of view that I most need my rights to be firmly entrenched, because I am then most at risk of being de-humanised or otherwise demonised.

[20] Aquinas *De Regno* 2, 11.

[21] In other words, returning to the reflections of John of Salisbury and many others.

[22] *Third Theological Oration on the Son II*

fully polycratic idea of transcendent laws does not provide a satisfactory answer for the kind of accountability to law that is needed.

On the other hand if we talk of a polycratic system in which the different centres of power and authority do ultimately relate to each other in an order hierarchy, then we have to all intents and purposes not only a system which holds people to account in a coherent way, but which is, at the end of the day, monarchical in the sense that there is an ordered set of priorities. We need to look at this possibility further.

If there is such a divine monarchy, we have to see how it is that the monarchical prerogatives of the Son are consistent rather than competitive with, or independent of, those of the Father. For it is the unity of the divine monarchy that contributes so decisively both to the certainty of salvation and also to the certainty of justice being rendered to earthly power-holders. We have just seen how defective the idea of polyarchy would be in the divine or transcendental sphere.

However, Moltmann is by no means atypical in his aversion to authority claims and his suspicion of them. This takes us to the way that post-Nietzschean thought reduces claims to love others to power claims, and correspondingly eliminates genuine love on the part of one who obeys someone in authority.

7.4   Love subsumed into power relations

7.4.1   Nietzsche and benevolent action as pursuing power

The American philosopher R Rorty is said to have commented that all philosophy is now Nietzschean. Certainly Nietzsche has articulated an approach that many have followed and which very intentionally tends to reduce all social relations to exercises of power. Thus Nietzsche argues for the equivalence of hurting and benefiting others. Both are ways of exercising power:

> *On the doctrine of the feeling of power* [=Machtgelüst]. – Benefiting and hurting others are ways of exercising one's power over them – that is all one wants in such cases! We *hurt* those to whom we need to make our power perceptible, the pain is a much more sensitive means to that end than pleasure: pain always asks for the cause, while pleasure is inclined to stop with itself and not look back. We *benefit* and show benevolence to those who already depend on us in some way (that is, who are used to thinking of us as their causes); we want to increase their power because we thus increase our own, or we want to show them the advantage of being in our power – that

way, they will be more satisfied with their situation and more hostile towards and willing to fight against the enemies of *our* power.[23]

As is well known, Nietzsche saw the fundamental motive force in life and certainly in human psychology as the will to power.[24] This means that even apparently selfless, non-power-seeking actions need to be interrogated for the way they in fact serve a power interest. One must be suspicious.

7.4.2   The eradication of other-personed love

This tendency to intense suspicion is perceptively and presciently caught by C S Lewis in his children's novel *The Last Battle* as he describes the reaction of some dwarfs to being rescued by Eustace and his friends:

> "Little beasts!" said Eustace. "Aren't you even going to say *thank you* for being saved from the salt-mines?"

> "Oh, we know all about that," said Griffle over his shoulder. "You wanted to make use of us, that's why you rescued us. You're playing some game of your own. Come on, you chaps."[25]

The tragedy here is that a genuine good has been done out of genuine compassion, but the dwarfs (Griffle and his companions) have a hermeneutical grid of suspicion that means that they genuinely cannot see what is there. Their *chic* cynicism leaves them unable to discern other-personed compassion directed to them from others. They are unloved, in a sense, because their preconceptions make them incapable of distinguishing other-personed love from selfishness. They cannot receive other-personed love for what it is. It is not that other-personed love is not offered.

Further, as those who are unloved in their own view, there is a tragic inevitability to their reaction towards others which is to say '...the dwarfs are for the dwarfs' – they will serve only themselves.[26] Not only are they unloved, but they are unable to love others than themselves. In this sense they are incapable and unwilling (both are true) to enter into the perfection of love that Richard of Saint Victor describes, which is a love

---

[23] *The Gay Science*, section 13. For similar descriptions see also *Beyond Good and Evil*, section 36.

[24] *Beyond Good and Evil* section 36. Nietzsche's emphasis on the will to power as the fundamental wellspring of action owes no little debt to A Schopenhauer's idea that the fundamental wellspring of action is the will to life.

[25] Lewis *The Last Battle* (London: HarperCollins, 2001) (1st published 1956) p 93.

[26] Lewis *The Last Battle* p 93.

for others, rather than a 'private love' of oneself by oneself. What is more, the eradication of any distinctive other-personed love inevitably means a certain shamelessness about such 'private love' – it is perceived as justified since, so to speak, everyone is at it.

7.4.3   Power as amoral

With this in mind we have to ask what impact this Nietzschean line of argument has on the discussion of the eternal subordination of the Son. The answer is intriguing.

We must remember that Nietzsche is no friend to conventional moral evaluation. Part of his disdain towards his contemporary culture was its attempts to hold on to Christian morality without believing in God. His analysis of harming and benefiting others as being equivalent acts in fact leads one readily to conclude that he was an amoralist on the exercise of power – an act of power was simply that: an act of power. That clearly followed once one analysed the well-spring of human action as actualisations of the will to power. Similarly Foucault has been criticised because he renders beyond moral evaluation actions which are repugnant, since they are, like all inter-personal actions, in the context of ongoing relations of war.[27]

But this means two things in the current debate. To begin with, within a Nietzschean framework one cannot say that any eternal subordination between Father and Son is a *wicked* power relation. It is just a power relation – 'beyond good and evil', so to speak.[28] Similarly, one cannot say that an egalitarian, non-subordination relation is somehow ethically *better* because it is more egalitarian. That, too, is 'beyond good and evil'. Nietzsche and Foucault would remind us that there is no such thing as an 'altruistic egalitarian relation' with others: that would just be another, possibly very subtle, way of pursuing power. It is important to grasp this: if Nietzsche and Foucault are right, then a purported egalitarian relationship is every bit as power-laden as an overtly hierarchical relationship. Far from supporting the arguments against subordination on the grounds that such relationships are power-laden, a Nietzschean approach regards subordination between ontological equals as merely another way of exercising power, and no better nor any worse than others ways of exercising power in relationships, including

---

[27]   Foucault demands 'Shouldn't one therefore conceive all problems of power in terms of relations of war?' Foucault, M 'Truth and Power' in Gordon, C (ed.) *Power/Knowledge* (New York: Pantheon, 1980) pp 122, 123.

[28]   To play with the title of one of Nietzsche's works.

purportedly egalitarian patterns. In fact, a purportedly egalitarian relationship can be more deceptive than an overtly ordered relationship since the former tends to hide its contours of power.

To this extent, the arguments of relational egalitarianism do not by themselves refute the Nietzschean case. In fact, Nietzschean suspicion unmasks the claims of relational egalitarianism to be ethically better. Of course, some relational egalitarians might say that the Nietzschean analysis does not apply to relations within the Trinity because they are by definition perfect relations. But this response is hardly unique to relational egalitarians: one can equally say (and one should) that an ordered Trinity with the eternal subordination of the Son is equally immune to Nietzsche's reductionist power ethic because the Father is morally perfect and therefore non-abusive in his use of authority.

7.5 The impact of denying the eternal subordination of the Son on power/authority claims

However, it is not at all clear that those asserting that the Son only obeys in his humanity are making precisely the same claim as Nietzsche and Foucault, that all relations are power relations and are to that extent equally amoral. Rather the force of attributing Arianism to those asserting the eternal subordination of the Son is that a key premise is held in common with the Arians, namely that relational subordination rules out ontological equality, and this is bad.

Of course, this premise might be applied in two different ways. Thus it could be used very generally to the effect that no personal entity is equal to another personal entity if it is relationally subordinate to that other entity. Alternatively, it could be used very specifically to the effect that no divine personal entity can be ontologically equal to another personal divine entity if it is relationally subordinate to that other entity. Yet both of these alternatives present problems for a biblical account of power and authority.

Thus, if one takes the general sense (namely, that no personal entity is equal to another personal entity if it is relationally subordinate), one is clearly faced with the issue that human children are told to honour and obey their parents. Similarly as citizens, Christians are enjoined to submit to even pagan civil authorities. These cases of human-human obedience and submission do not mean that parents or rulers are on a higher ontological level. In fact, as we have seen, Nicene theology actually uses the fact of obedience within human sonship to argue for ontological equality. This means that if we were to accept the premise in this general sense, we have undercut a good many biblically warranted notions of power/authority. At that stage one is led to ask where this premise actually comes from. It certainly leaves one asking when power/authority is ever legitimate. As we have seen, the logic of Moltmann's 'kingdom without a lord' position is precisely that any authority becomes inherently suspect. We have already seen the difficulties the Moltmann thesis faces with regard to the use of 'Abba' in the Gethsemane prayer.

This leaves the more narrow version of the premise about ontological equality, namely that which stipulates that it is only in the case of divine persons that ontological equality rules out relational subordination. There are several difficulties here. Obviously one is inclined to ask where this principle is given within the biblical testimony, either explicitly, or by good and necessary consequence. But in the present context, we should note that this draws a very sharp divide at the ethical level between the exercise of power/authority in creation and how it works within the Trinity in eternity. After all, eternal Trinitarian relations are perfect: perfectly loving and perfectly good at the ethical level. But the thrust of the premise in this form means that those perfect personal relations in eternity are not mirrored in human-human relations. In fact the relation between civil ruler and citizen is exactly *not* like the intra-Trinitarian relations in eternity. On that basis, an obvious question is how such human-human relations which do involve power/authority can ever be good and loving, either on the part of the ruler or on the part of the ruled.

This means that whether we follow the Nietzschean line of argument or indeed the eternal relational egalitarian line or Moltmann's line, we are left with some severe questions about how other-personed love and authority can possibly fit together. These questions about other-personed love are compounded as we consider other aspects of the late modern situation.

7.6   Late modern misgivings about hierarchy

7.6.1   Individual and collective

Trinitarian doctrine inevitably focuses on personal relationship and this is extremely pertinent for a culture born in late capitalism, as ours is, for late capitalism creates particular pressures for individual persons.[29] Notably there is the risk of both a toxic individualism and a toxic totalism which tends to subsume the distinctiveness of the individual (C Gunton envisaged that not only could the two co-exist but that they could even paradoxically feed off each other).

7.6.1.1   Individuals as uniform individual agents of consumption

Thus, one current cultural strand is an untrammelled individualism in which each seeks to maximise his or her own 'utility' (understood in J Bentham's sense of the seeking of pleasure and the avoidance of pain).[30] Each is considered as a mature individual who is the best judge of his or her best interest.[31] This pleasure/pain can become so individualised that another's pain (for example, working in an overseas sweatshop to make consumer goods for the West) is irrelevant for my pleasure.[32]

But that impulse to individualism co-exists with another powerful trend: an individualism without full individuation. By this we mean an individualism where people are numerically individual, but are essentially interchangeable with each other. There are many individuals, perhaps, but uniform individuals. Thus, the much-vaunted ability of internet engines to 'profile' individual users looks like a species of individuation, but the basis on which this is done individuates me as a

---

[29]   One notes here especially the work of the late Colin Gunton.

[30]   Bentham writes: 'Nature has placed mankind under the governance of two sovereign masters, *pain* and *pleasure*. It is for them alone to point out what we ought to do, as well as to determine what we shall do.' *An Introduction to the Principles of Morals and Legislation* I.I. (1907) Clarendon: Oxford(1st published 1789.).

[31]   This theme of the mature judgment of the enlightened individual is fundamental to I Kant's justification for repudiating 'authority' in his 1784 essay 'What is Enlightenment?' and feeds through into the vital presupposition of J S Mill's *On Liberty* (2006)   Harmondsworth: Penguin (1st published 1859) that each individual is the best judge of his or her own interest.

[32]   J S Mill's 'no harm' principle assumes that another's pain is relevant for my consideration. But, of course, individual hedonism gives no ground for this assumption. Two significant difficulties at least surround the 'no harm' principle: first, who defines what 'harm' is; secondly, when does my omission (for example not protesting about two-thirds world textile workers' conditions) become harm – or is harm only a positive action? This, though, would take Mill close to thinking about duty and he prefers to think about rights.

consumer.[33] I have preferences for these dvds rather than those, I buy these goods online rather than those and so on. But the vital thing here is not which dvds I buy (my personal preference is not relevant in itself), but that I buy some dvds.

Yet I may well feel that there is more to me as an individual than my consumer preferences: this basis of individuation trivialises me, even while granting me importance as a consumer, but one might say, only as a consumer. The trivialisation occurs because those aspects of my individual identity which stand outside my consumer preferences (for instance a commitment to protection for political prisoners) tend either to be unrecognised altogether, or translated into something that is commodified and consumable, as when I am asked what economic value I place on my commitment to protect political prisoners. This process of commodification trivialises these things by rendering them things that only matter insofar as they translate into something else, into economic consumable value. Economic consumability is the common denominator, or perhaps the universal solvent. Since these things have value only when and in so far as translated into economic consumable terms, they start to look necessarily secondary, rather than primary.

There again, if I am myself primarily only a consumer, and my preferences are increasingly commodified, then I will be increasingly led to regard the external world as existing for my consumption: it is there for me, not I for it, nor even are we there for each other. A society premised on untrammelled individualism understood as consumption is going to struggle desperately with an idea of love that sees love of others as primary and not as basically an indirect means of self-satisfaction.[34] We have already noted Richard of St Victor's comment that perfect love was a good deal more than, and very different in orientation from, a 'private love of oneself'. But a strongly individualist culture along the lines the West has adopted has little basis on which to argue for the importance, let alone the priority, of other-person centred love. The persistent tendency is to translate other-personed love back into something that is self-serving.

---

[33] Compare the insight of J Baudrillard that late capitalist culture does de-humanise, just as earlier capitalism did, but on a different basis: where earlier capitalism saw the individual fundamentally as a unit of production, late capitalism sees the individual as a unit of consumption.

[34] What one might call a will to pleasure rather than a will to power.

This, naturally, relates us back again to that striking feature of the late modern/post-modern western cultural mood that we have explored above in terms of Nietzsche and Foucault– its hermeneutics of suspicion, including its suspicion of claims or attempts to act in goodness towards others.

7.6.1.2   Individuals as ENTITLED agents of consumption

This idea of individual as consumer further relates closely to the cultural trends analysed by J M Twenge and others to the effect that the modern cultural west is increasingly an entitlement, or narcissistic, culture in which the individual is increasingly encouraged to love him or herself as an entitlement.[35] The strain of narcissism Twenge describes can take quite aggressive forms, demanding as of right from those around a person because of that person's sense of intrinsic, automatic and unearned self-importance.[36] Twenge and W K Campbell perceptively speak of rearing children now as 'raising royalty' – royalty are simply entitled by virtue of being born.[37] Love for others is not always denied here, but takes second place to, and indeed, so the argument goes, can really only properly arise from a prior love of self.[38] One must love oneself before being able to love others. Relationships with others become fundamentally ways of serving oneself. Twenge and Campbell contrast the narcissist approach to personal relationships with older more other-person centred ideas:

> In place of caring, put exploitation; and to commitment add "as long as it benefits me." Narcissists' approach to relationships is simple: it's all about them. They want to look and feel good, and if the relationship is a way to do this, great; if not, it's time to find another.[39]

---

[35] Lasch, C *The Culture of Narcissism* (New York: W. Norton, 1978) also speaks of a narcissistic culture, but in a slightly different sense – his 'narcissist' is characterised by a certain neediness: he writes of a personality: '... immediately recognizable, in a more subdued form, to observers of the contemporary cultural scene: facile at managing the impressions he gives to others, ravenous for admiration but contemptuous of those he manipulates into providing it; unappeasably hungry for emotional experiences with which to fill an inner void; terrified of aging and death.'

[36] Twenge, J M *Generation Me* (New York: Free Press, 2007), Twenge, J M and Campbell, W K *The Narcissism Epidemic: Living in the Age of Entitlement* (New York: Free Press, 2009).

[37] Twenge and Campbell *Narcissism Epidemic.*

[38] Twenge and Campbell do not subscribe to this argument but note its importance.

[39] Twenge and Campbell *Narcissism Epidemic* p 213.

To this extent, the late capitalist West, while it has what is in many ways a laudable stress on individual liberty, also has an account of the individual with some remarkable and incoherent features. The individual is an 'entitled' agent of consumption, but is also one who, to the outside observer, lacks individuation, for one consumer is interchangeable with another. But each entitled, consuming individual has been increasingly encultured to see himself or herself as somehow unique. It does not take much to see that this account of the individual is remarkably unstable – how can each person be a uniquely entitled agent of consumption? – as well as prone to encouraging a sinful self-centredness and self-service. One may add the practical but important critique that Twenge and Campbell frequently recite – narcissistic entitlement stands at odds with reality and is calculated to nurture rage, depression, sadness and grievance.[40]

7.6.1.3 Agents of consumption in a collectivist enterprise – as 'last men'

However, the lack of a principle of individuation that is not trivialising creates other pressures too. If the individual is basically an economic agent of consumption, then it is tempting for both corporate agencies, whether capitalist or state, to treat this mass of individual agents as a total group that one can affect, influence, tax, and if necessary penalise. Hence Gunton's fear that, in a strongly individualist but not well-individuated society, one would be dealing with people who had been made into a 'mass', and one can compare also Nietzsche's fear that modern society would become a conglomeration not of supermen but of 'ultimate men'.[41]

Such 'ultimate men' are etiolated and enervated products of the culture Nietzsche saw developing around him and are unable to 'give birth to any star', but rather 'make everything small', culminating in Nietzsche's contemptuous comment about mass democratic culture:

> No Shepherd, and one herd! Everyone wanteth the same; everyone is equal: he who hath other sentiments goes voluntarily into

---

[40] See Twenge *Generation Me* and Twenge and Campbell *Narcissism Epidemic*. Twenge *Generation Me* points in particular to the anger an entitlement narcissist characteristically can display when his or her perceived entitlements are denied. It stands at odds with reality because, contrary to the entitlement mantra 'you can be what you want to be', not all of us can be international standard opera singers no matter what endeavours we make, again a point that Twenge makes.

[41] The 'last man' or the 'ultimate man' is explored notably in *Thus Spoke Zarathustra*.

the madhouse.[42]

What is more, those exercising authority in such a culture would themselves have been socialised into a strongly individualist ethic of consumption, in which power becomes another means for individual consumption. Hence Gunton's well-taken fears that the paradoxical long-term consequence of individualist consumption would be a totalising/totalitarian political structure. The consumption spin, of course, means that the primary political good becomes the preservation and promotion of a consumption economy and issues of equality etc. are finally only means to achieve that and thus can be jettisoned or modified if not serving that end.

In more traditional theological terms, Gunton and others were observing that the authority structures and social organisation in such individualist cultures essentially will come to mirror and, fatally to inculcate, a humanity *incurvatus in se* (curved in on itself), with a disordered love of self, and a consequently disordered love of others.

7.6.1.4 Authority and 'incurvatus in se'

These factors bear heavily on that singularly striking feature of current late modern culture, the authority question. On the one hand, as J Habermas and others consistently point out, there is a remarkably anti-authoritarian stream in modern western attitudes, while on the other hand there is a proliferation of laws and regulations – this is a highly regulated yet in some ways anti-authoritarian society.[43]

This in turn poses a profound question about the moral value of obedience. For there is, understandably, a strand within contemporary anti-authoritarianism that sees rebellion against authority as morally virtuous and, in a sense, heroic. Indeed, Christian political theology of the John of Salisbury type would say that under certain conditions rebellion is indeed morally virtuous. Yet the question becomes whether one sees **all** acts of anti-authority as necessarily heroic. Russian anarchist Mikhail Bakunin set the tone for this necessarily heroic stance in writing:

> Man has emancipated himself; he has separated himself from animality and constituted himself a man; he has begun his

---

[42] All these references come from *Thus Spoke Zarathustra* prologue 5.

[43] One needs to say 'in some ways' because there are also counter-vailing tendencies towards silencing dissenting opinion. The obvious example is the 'political correctness' area.

distinctively human history and development by an act of disobedience and science – that is, by *rebellion* and by *thought*. 44

Within this framework of thought, obedience appears not just craven but deserving moral condemnation.45 This includes obedience to God.46 This revulsion at 'craven obedience' to God has been present for some time within our culture: it is, of course, described by Milton as he depicts Satan's revolt in *Paradise Lost*. But it is actually celebrated in Shelley's *Prometheus Unbound* and put at a popular level in P Pullman's recent *His Dark Materials* series. Pullman's point is that we want a 'Republic of Heaven', not the 'Kingdom of God'. The two fold nature of Pullman's change is significant: 'republic' in place of 'kingdom'; and 'Heaven' in place of 'God'.

However, traditional western theology in Augustine's tradition would want to be far more nuanced over rebellion than this. As we have seen there are times when a tyrannical regime is in power and then, so western theologians insist, it may be indeed right to depose the tyrant.47 Yet rebellion may also be done from bad motives.48 Thus rebellion in Genesis 3 is neither good, nor grateful nor justified. It is prompted above all by a disordered love of self, arising ultimately from pride. This means that just as there is obviously a wrong use of authority by the power-holder that is bound up with pride and self-incurvature (*incurvatus in se* in the traditional language), so too there may be a refusal of authority by the one subject to authority that is prompted by disordered love of self at the expense of love of others. In this way there is a false self-serving heroism to the rebellion against the Lord's Anointed of Psalm 2:2-3. The horrendous nature of this rebellion by humanity is fully revealed in Acts as we are told that the Crucifixion was the fulfilment of the Psalm 2:2-3 rebellion (Acts 4:25-27) and that this rebellion was a siding by us with Death against the Lord of Life (Acts 3:14-15).

One might then say that part of Bakunin's tragedy is that his singular alertness to the abuse of power by the self-loving power-holder

---

44 Bakunin, M *God and the State*. (New York: Mother Earth Publishing Association, 1916).
45 Compare the implications of Kant, 'What is Enlightenment?' (1784) on the 'mature' who wish to remain 'under authority'.
46 Bakunin thinks God inevitably demands obedience and for that reason must cease to be.
47 Certainly disobedience may be right. The book of Daniel features repeated and various degrees of disobedience to a presumptuous and overweening civil power.
48 David does not lift his hand against the Lord's anointed.

has left him blind to the possibility of a wrong self-love prompting rebellion. He is unable to conceive that Adam and Eve are ethically wrong in Genesis 3.[49] He also cannot conceive that the murder of Jesus the Son was unrighteous. It is intriguing to ask where the possibility of wrongful refusal of authority even finds a place in much contemporary discourse, with the significant but self-interested exception of wrongly refusing the voice of the majority.

It is, however, important to observe here that the New Testament does indeed teach obedience in certain relationships, in what is to our culture's eyes a very unfashionable way. Obviously some relationships which might feature authority are currently strongly contested,[50] but it remains relatively non-controversial to envisage that the New Testament teaches authority in the relation of citizen and state and between church leader and congregation. What is more, in the relationship between the citizen and the state, obedience is not only enjoined (Romans 13:1ff, 1 Peter 2:13-18) but is indeed treated as a Christian virtue. Yet obviously it has become highly problematic to see obedience (as against agreement) as a *virtue* in this anti-authoritarian culture.

What is even more striking is that in biblical terms obedience is not only a virtue but is also related to love. This occurs in two dimensions: in one dimension there is a law that we love one another (e.g. 1 John 3:11; 2 John 5). Here the content of the law is that we are to love each other. But in another dimension we obey Jesus' commandments because we love him (John 14:15). To this extent obedience to Jesus is born out of love for him and the virtue of obedience and the relationship of love are not mutually exclusive but actually joined together. Love for Jesus engenders and motivates obedience to him. Correspondingly, lack of obedience to Jesus suggests lack of love for him.

As we articulate this, it is immediately apparent that this fits very poorly with the analysis of power and authority that Nietzsche and others provide. If benefiting others is a tool of my power, then obedience likewise is not a virtue, nor is it other-personed love. This sits so clearly at odds with the New Testament that one has to ask how it can be corrected. Clearly on the Moltmann view, obedience cannot be love, since logically it should not exist within his redefined 'kingdom without a lord'. But likewise with the view that ontological equality precludes

---

49 As becomes very clear in Bakunin *God and the State* as he comments on Genesis 3.
50 Notably a husband's headship within marriage.

submission, one needs to ask how, where there is an authority relationship, it can be virtuous and reciprocally loving, with other-personed love both on the part of the one in authority and on the part of the one who is obedience.

There is a lurking sting here in the argument that authority/power precludes ontological equality between power-holder and those in obedience. If we think this principle is true, and if we think that the Bible does teach that, say, there is legitimate authority in the state, then one should logically conclude that the power-holder is of a higher ontological nature than the one who is obedient. This is deeply problematic because, far from protecting us from the abuse of power by power-holders, this premise of those arguing against the Son's eternal subordination actually serves to insulate the power-holder from proper challenge by those over whom power is held. Such people who are under power are, after all, ontologically inferior on this line of argument. At this stage, of course, this form of the argument against the Son's eternal subordination tends to merge with Moltmann's view, or else it starts to treat the holding of power as in itself conferring ontological superiority. As observed before, this moves perilously close to the worship of power.

7.6.2   Virtue and obedience

This relates to an even more theologically central question, that of humility, which certainly is not the worship of power. In what way does our contemporary culture endorse humility, with its consequent preferential treatment by me of others as outlined in Philippians 2, as a **virtue**? Humility in Philippians 2:1ff involves a treatment of others that is the antithesis of treating others as if I am an entitled consumer. Humility does not stand on entitlement, nor does it treat others and their resources as being there fundamentally for my consumption.

7.6.2.1   Obedience and delegated authority

Further, Romans 13 is clear that I obey the state for my God's sake. I obey him and therefore obey his delegates. The delegates themselves only have a relative authority.[51] And therefore, when, as Daniel found, the voice of the state and the voice of God clash, the higher authority lies with God. I listen to him first, as the 1934 Barmen Declaration made

---

[51]   As we have seen above this delegation of authority and the consequent limitations this imposes on an authority that is only delegated is largely under-stated by Moltmann.

clear.[52] To the state, of course, this will look today like the worst kind of sedition – but then it did in 1934.

To this extent, in this phase of later modernity, Christians are doubly counter-cultural on the authority question. This doubly counter-cultural orientation is not always appreciated (in any sense). First, Christians traditionally see obedience and humility as virtues related to other-personed love, not unpleasant necessities. This can attract hostility from those who wish to adopt an anti-authoritarian stance, at least on some issues. Christian obedience and humility can be seen as unduly quietist and likely to make one a doormat.[53]

However, Christians are also counter-cultural in seeing God rather than human authority as having the prior claim on our loyalty and obedience. This priority on the claims of God is seen in the refusal by our forebears in the early church to engage in emperor-worship, but is also seen in rejecting today the claim that the democratic majoritarian state has the prior claim to our loyalty. When Christians are counter-cultural in this way, they are naturally seen as disorderly, subversive and somewhat anarchistic.

This means paradoxically, in the climate of the modern cultural west which has features of both entitlement individualism and also 'totalitarian democracy', Christians who stress loving obedience to God can seem to that culture both authoritarian and anarchistic.

Further, a key pastoral question for us as we live in this culture is how we are to conceive of authority, whether it is possible both to hold authority and also to love those over whom one holds it, and whether it is possible both to be under authority and also to love those who have authority over one.

7.6.2.2   The place of virtue in God

The virtue question is further complicated by how one conceives of the goodness of God. A strong and venerable stream of Christian theology

---

[52]   The first 'evangelical truth' of the Barmen Declaration reads, after citing John 14:6 and 10:1 and 9:

Jesus Christ, as he is attested for us in holy scripture, is the one Word of God which we have to hear and which we have to trust and obey in life and in death.

We reject the false doctrine, as though the church could and would have to acknowledge as a source of its proclamation, apart from and besides this one Word of God, still other events and powers, figures and truths, as God's revelation.

[53]   This criticism of humility as a virtue goes right back to the antipathy some in the Greco-Roman world felt towards 'humility'.

sees God as the source of all the kinds of goodness and virtue that there are in creation. He is the source not only of the world's existence but of its goodness.[54] As this source, he has **all** the virtues *perfectly*.[55] Since he has his attributes perfectly and completely, it is not enough to say he has justice and love as attributes, he *is* justice and he *is* love in that he has those attributes completely and perfectly: every aspect of love and justice which is found as scattered individual and separate instances within creation is found in him fully and together.

The problem this raises, of course, in the context of humility and obedience is whether these are virtues that are not found eternally in the triune creator God but only in his creatures. Can we as creatures have a virtue that God our creator does not? This bears profoundly on how important we think these virtues are. If we have a virtue that God does not, then naturally one is inclined to ask quite how significant it is. And yet we can see that a consistent theme (perhaps especially in Luke-Acts) is that God opposes the proud and mercifully lifts up the humble.

Here we need to return to Augustine for whom the humility/pride dichotomy was so central. There are grounds for thinking that Augustine saw the Son's humility as extending beyond his human nature. Thus in commenting on Philippians 2:6-7, he writes:

> Nonetheless, though he did not regard equality with God as something belonging to another, but to himself, he emptied himself, not looking out for his interests, but for ours. So that you may know that this is true, pay attention to how the apostle came to his point. He was teaching Christians the humility present in love.[56]

Augustine's point here is that outside the Incarnation the Son was fully equal to the Father but at that point emptied himself. This suggests that the Son did not become humble because he had taken human nature. Rather he took human nature because he is eternally humble.

A related issue is that for Augustine humility is linked with love of others. This helps us see humility too in the love of the Father, for with other-personed and unenvious love he wants his Son to be equally honoured with himself. This is the same kind of regard for others which

---

[54] Anselm *Monologion* I.

[55] Much of this discussion begins with Anselm's *Monologion* (but see also his *Proslogion*), although the thought of God as being perfect goodness is clearly present in patristic theologians such as Athanasius and Lactantius.

[56] *Answer to Maximinus* I, V see also *Answer to Maximinus* II XV,I.

Paul commands for the Philippians at the beginning of chapter 2 of his letter. The particular form that the Father's humility to his Son takes may be distinctively paternal but it expresses the general principle of other-personed regard and love.

This is of singular importance for our understanding of the character of the triune God. Our post-modern mood rightly resonates with the critique of self-serving power-seeking that the Augustinian tradition offers in its depiction of human disordered self-love, humanity curved in on itself. The vice of pride is intimately involved in this kind of will-to-power narcissism. But we have seen how Augustine also puts pride as the antithesis of humility.[57] It is therefore of the greatest comfort and significance to realise that the Persons of the Trinity manifest in their eternal relationships with each other not pride and self-love but humility and other-personed love and regard. This humility and other-personed love takes place within the context of the intra-Trinitarian personal relationships, so that the Son loves as a son, the Father as a father and so forth: to this extent the different individual loves are manifested in different ways.

Conversely, if loving, other-personed humility is not found within the eternal relations, one may start to downplay the significance of self-serving disordered self-love. If God is not humble, would he then be proud?

7.7 The contribution of the eternal subordination of the Son

However, it may well be asked how a Trinitarian theology incorporating the eternal subordination of the Son contributes to these very pressing problems of late modern western culture. This occurs in several dimensions.

7.7.1 The uniqueness of the persons

We have seen that one of the issues with the individualism of our culture is that while it insists on a numerical individualism, such that while you the reader and I the writer are both individuals, we are nevertheless not individuated: that is, we are interchangeable and uniform rather than unique.

---

57 *Tractate on John* XXV.16.

Here we should be grateful to Augustine's stress that the Trinity is not a society of three friends, but Father, Son and Spirit. His point was that the Persons of the Trinity are unique because the relations in which they stand to one another are unique. The Son relates to the Father as Son not as Father, nor as friend to friend. We distort the biblical revelation if we obscure the asymmetry of the relations between the Persons. But it is precisely the asymmetry that establishes the uniqueness of the Persons of the Trinity such that they are not a society of three symmetrical and interchangeable friends.

Yet the risk of the relational egalitarian case is that it may obscure exactly this asymmetry and therefore undercut the unique, individuated nature of the Persons in their relations to one another. It is very natural for us to think in terms of 'three friends' as the relevant pattern when we hear the claim of relational egalitarianism. Indeed, friendship is rightly valued in contemporary culture, not least because contemporary friendship has a strong egalitarian dimension to it.[58] But it is not what is revealed in the Incarnation, and Tertullian reminds us that we must deal with what has been revealed rather than what we think might have been the case.

Of course, a responsible relational egalitarian will immediately say that we must preserve the asymmetry of Son and Father and Spirit. This is commendable, but if we assert asymmetry, we have to ask 'what goes into that asymmetry and on what basis?' The answer of John's Gospel is that the Father gives to the Son and sends the Son and the Son does his Father's will as a good biblical son should. Jesus the Son is a true son.

To this extent, the eternal subordination of the Son is part of the relational asymmetry which establishes the three Persons as unique. And their eternal uniqueness, as Gunton foresaw, underpins our uniqueness as human individuals who matter precisely because we are not interchangeable with each other but each uniquely in the image and likeness of God.

7.7.2   *Love, authority and obedience*

We have also noted during this survey of modern conditions that there are current arguments that relate love, authority and obedience badly.

---

[58]   Interestingly earlier generations would not necessarily see friendship as having an inherently egalitarian element: in the novels of Jane Austen, for example, friendship exists between members of different social classes, but the reality of those class distinctions is not denied.

POWER, INDIVIDUALISM AND VIRTUE

Thus some say that love is merely one way of exercising power and authority in a fundamentally self-serving way and this is ethically neutral. Others suggest that love and authority are simply antithetical and exclude each other: neither the authority-holder nor the one subject to authority can truly and ethically love the other. This is deeply problematic for two reasons. First, so much of the biblical testimony does speak of a God who has authority and secondly, human social organisation requires some kind of account of power that does not simply say all power is evil.[59]

In fact, a Trinitarian account of the eternal subordination of the Son does allow us to speak of love, authority and obedience as properly joined rather than as separated or subsumed.

7.7.2.1   Love and authority

Thus with regard to the Father, we note the stress of the Johannine Jesus that his Father loves him and in consequence of that has given him all things and has sent him into the world. Jesus does not think his Father's authority in doing the things his Father has commanded – even when that includes the Cross – is inconsistent with his Father's love for him.

We might, of course, follow a Nietzschean line here and suggest Jesus has been deceived about his Father's true motives and intentions. The disadvantage of this approach is that it presupposes that Jesus does not know his Father truly and exhaustively. It rests, in other words, on a denial that Jesus is the true Son of the Father and indwells him and knows him perfectly. This undermines the revelation Jesus brings in areas that go far beyond the question of authority. Put sharply, the eternal subordination of the Son shows us that love and holding authority can go together.

7.7.2.2   Love and obedience

Likewise, the Son is clear that he loves his Father and shows this by his obedience. Obedience is therefore not necessarily produced by servile fear, nor is it simply a product of amoral power dynamics. Again, if one were to argue a Niezschean line that Jesus does not understand that his love is servile or a product of manipulation, then one would have

---

59   The teaching of Romans 13 does envisage the state as an agent for good at least in a relative sense in a fallen world. The word 'requires' in terms of an analysis of authority in ways that do not simply see it as always evil in every respect is therefore warranted.

undermined Jesus as the revealer of God anyway. For Jesus, his obedience is a matter of love. This is eternally the case if we accept the eternal subordination of the Son to the Father.

7.7.3   Re-configuring the criticisms

Taken together this means that a Trinitarian account which does feature the eternal subordination of the Son is able to provide an account of the asymmetry between the Persons that the Bible shows and can also ground proper authority/power in love. We need to stress that this does not give open season to abuses of power. The fears of the post-moderns about the abuse of power are very clearly by no means all ill-taken. But this consideration of the Trinitarian relations enables us to deconstruct power claims along slightly different lines than the post-moderns– how does this power/authority claim show love for the other? For, whether in exercising authority or in submitting to it, our responses to power/authority must be genuinely other-person centred. It is an appropriate and searching question whether a power-holder has exercised his/her power in other-person centred love and concluding that they have sinned if they have not. In this way there is an appropriate 'hermeneutics of suspicion'. But equally it is appropriate to ask whether a refusal to obey is prompted by a love of self rather than a love of others. Is it always loving others to refuse to obey someone whom the Bible says I should? But then, Augustine foresaw this issue long ago. Writing about the two different kinds of love, manifested in the two different 'cities',[60] he stated:

> We see then that the two cities were created by two kinds of love: the earthly city was created by self-love reaching the point of contempt for God, the Heavenly City by the love of God carried as far as contempt of self. In fact, the earthly city glories in itself, the Heavenly City glories in the Lord. The former looks for glory from men, the latter finds its highest glory in God, the witness of a good conscience. The earthly lifts up its head in its own glory, the Heavenly City says to its God: 'My glory; you lift up my head.' In the former, the lust for domination lords it over its princes as over the nations it subjugates; in the other both those put in authority and those subject to them serve one another in love, the rulers by their counsel, the subjects by obedience. The one city loves its own strength shown in its powerful leaders; the other says to its God. 'I

---

[60] The two 'cities' describe two different ways of human life in society.

will love you, my Lord, my strength.[61]

In this moving depiction, we note especially the phrases:

> ... in the other both those put in authority and those subject to them serve one another in love, the rulers by their counsel, the subjects by obedience.

On the eternal subordination view, loving authority and loving obedience can be rooted in the character of the eternal triune God. It is less clear that it can be so rooted on other views.

---

[61] Augustine *City of God* XIV.28

8   Concluding reflections

We have seen there are excellent reasons for seeing the subordination of the Son as something attested by key Nicene theologians. Their rationale comes within the framework of the preservation of the unity of the divine monarchy and the reality of the sonship of Jesus the Son. In that way it is consistent with pre-Nicene Trinitarian theology. Athanasius and Hilary have robust and coherent reasons for saying the Son's subordination is not Arian. The Son's subordination arises from the reality of his sonship and his personal relationship as son with his Father. It does not arise from him being a creature, as the Arians contended. Certainly care is needed in formulating the eternal subordination of the Son lest it detract from the eternal and unchanging character of the relations between the Father and the Son, as Basil and Augustine both saw. Since an eternal subordination affirms the eternal true sonship of the Son and denies that he is a creature, the charge of Arianism is ill-founded.

Instead we have seen how these Nicene views are biblically founded on considerations of the sending, giving and love motifs between Father and Son found in John's Gospel. Augustine relates the obedient love of the Son to his humility: this helpfully shapes our understanding of the eternal subordination in terms of this relational virtue: the eternal subordination of the Son is not so much something he does as the way he relates in eternal loving humility to his Father, which is manifested by obedience in the Incarnation. We have also seen how the Son's eternal subordination preserves the unity of his Person as we discuss the way he genuinely has two natures yet is one unified and coherent Person. As such, those making the charge of Arianism in the way we have examined should repent of it.

We should note some ramifications of rejecting these views. To begin with, if we reject the eternal subordination of the Son as son, this does not protect us from Arianism, but rather it re-introduces precisely the key question the Arians posed, which echoes the objections to Jesus by his opponents in John's Gospel, of how Father and Son can be one God. Asserting that the Son only obeys in his human nature means that the issue the Bible stresses as so important, how God is still one, remains unanswered with respect to the eternal relations. Secondly, at the level of method, denial of the Son's eternal subordination leaves us asserting that the relations of the immanent Trinity are not those of the economic Trinity. In principle this seems to open the door to preferring current ideologies of father-son relations to those revealed to us. Thirdly, if we restrict the obedience of the Son to his human nature only, this risks producing an internal contradiction within the Person of the Son as he wills different and inconsistent things in his human and divine natures. Fourthly, this rejection risks obscuring the character of the love between Father and Son, notably the humble beauty of the Son's loving obedience to his Father. It is good to talk of the intra-Trinitarian love, but this 'love' is not of course a blank cheque: it must be filled in on the terms of what is biblically revealed to us in the Incarnation. Fifthly, as a question of observation, rejecting the Son's eternal subordination as son means we still have no answer to one of the pressing questions of late capitalist western culture – namely whether power relationships are inherently sinful and whether humility and obedience can ever be good and loving or must necessarily be dehumanising. An inevitable question then arises from an Augustinian point of view: is our difficulty over obedience and subordination related to our more basic rejection of humility in favour of pride?

9   Bibliography and Index

9.1   *ANCIENT AND MEDIAEVAL WORKS*

Aquinas *De Regno* (ed Kenny, J.)

Athanasius *Contra Arianos*. Bright, W. (text) 1884 2nd ed. Oxford: Clarendon.
Atkinson, M. (trans.) *Nicene and Post-Nicene Fathers* 2nd series Vol. IV.
Schaff, P. and Wace H. (eds) repr. 1975 Grand Rapids: Eerdmans.

-----.   *Contra Gentes*. Thomson, R.W. (text and trans) 1971. Oxford: Clarendon.

-----.   *De Decretis*. Text: *Library of the Greek Fathers and Ecclesiastical Writers: Athanasius the Great* vol. 3. 1962. Athens. Newman, J.H. (trans) *Nicene and Post-Nicene Fathers* 2nd series Vol. IV. Schaff, P. and Wace H. (eds) repr. 1975 Grand Rapids: Eerdmans.

-----.   *De Incarnatione*. Thomson, R.W. (text and trans) 1971. Oxford: Clarendon.

-----.   *De Synodis*. Text: *Library of the Greek Fathers and Ecclesiastical Writers: Athanasius the Great* vol. 3. 1962. Athens. Newman, J.H. (trans) Robertson, A. (rev) *Nicene and Post-Nicene Fathers* 2nd series Vol. IV. Schaff, P. and Wace H. (eds) repr. 1975 Grand Rapids: Eerdmans.

Augustine *Answer to an Arian Sermon*. Teske, R.J., (trans) 1995. New York: New City Press.

-----.   *Answer to Maximinus*. Teske, R.J. (trans) 1995. New York: New City Press.

-----.   *De Trinitate*. Hill, E. (trans) 1991. New York: New City Press.

-----.   *Debate with Maximinus*. Teske, R.J. (trans) 1995. New York: New City Press.

-----.   *Heresies*. Teske, R.J. (trans) 1995. New York: New City Press.

Basil the Great *De Spiritu Sancto*

-----.,   Letter VIII *To the Caesareans*

Gaius (1958) *Institutes* text F. de Zulueta. Oxford: Clarendon Press.

Gregory of Nazianzen   *Third Theological Oration*

-----.,   *Fourth theological Oration*

Hilary of Poitiers *De Synodis Nicene and Post-Nicene Fathers* Pullan, L. (trans) 2nd series Vol. IX. Schaff, P. (ed) repr. 1976 Grand Rapids: Eerdmans.

-----.   *De Trinitate* Text: Smulders, P. 2001.Paris: Cerf. Watson, Bennett, E.N. and Gayford, S.C. (trans) *Nicene and Post-Nicene Fathers* 2nd series Vol. IX. Schaff, P. (ed) repr. 1976 Grand Rapids: Eerdmans.

Hippolytus *Against Noetus*. Butterworth, R. (text and trans) 1977. London: Heythrop Monographs.

John of Salisbury (1159) *Policraticus*

Justinian. (1948) *Institutes*. [text] T.C. Sandars. London: Longmans Green and Co.

Origen. *Dialogue with Heraclides*. Chadwick, H. (trans) 1954. in *Alexandrian Christianity* Vol. II of Library of Christian Classics. London: SCM.

-----.   *On First Principles*. Crombie, F. (trans) *Ante-Nicene Fathers* Vol. IV Roberts, A. and Donaldson, J. (eds) repr. 1968 Grand Rapids: Eerdmans.

Salutati, C. *De Tyranno*

Tertullian *Against Hermogenes.* Waszink, J.H. (trans) 1956. ACW 24 New
     York/Ramsey: Newman Publishing.
-----.   *Against Marcion.* Holmes, P. (trans) *Ante-Nicene Fathers* Vol. III
     Roberts, A. and Donaldson, J. (eds) repr. 1968 Grand Rapids:
     Eerdmans.
-----.   *Against Praxeas.* Evans, E. (text and trans) 1948.London: SPCK.
-----.   *On Idolatry.* Waszink, J.H. and Van Winden, J.C.M. (text and trans)
     1987. Leiden: Brill.

9.2   MODERN WORKS

Adam, P. (2005). 'Honouring Jesus Christ', *Churchman*, 35-50.
Ayres, L. (2004). *Nicaea and its Legacy: An approach to Fourth-Century
     Trinitarian Theology.* Oxford: OUP.
Bakunin, M. (1916). *God and the State.* New York: Mother Earth Publishing
     Association.
Bathrellos, D. (2004). *The Byzantine Christ: Person, Nature, and Will in the
     Christology of Maximus the Confessor* Oxford: OUP.
Barrett, C.K. (1962) *The Gospel According to John* London: SPCK.
Beckwith, C. (2008). *Hilary of Poitiers on the Trinity: from De Fide to De
     Trinitate.* Oxford: OUP.
Bentham, J. (1907) *An Introduction to the Principles of Morals and Legislation*
     Clarendon: Oxford. (1st published 1789).
Bilezikian, G., 1997. 'Hermeneutical Bungee-Jumping: Subordination in the
     Godhead' *JETS* 40.1:57-68.
Blichner, L. and Molander, A (2005) 'What is Juridification?' Centre for
     European Studies (Oslo), working paper 14, 2005.
Bolt, P. (2005) 'Three Heads in the Divine Order: The Early church Fathers
     and 1 Corinthians 11:3' *RTR* vol 64:147-161.
Borgen, P. 1970. 'God's Agent in the Fourth Gospel' pp 137-148 in Neusner, J.
     (ed.) *Religions in Antiquity.* Leiden: Brill.
Brown, R.E.,(1971) *The Gospel According to John* Anchor (2 vols) London:
     Geoffrey Chapman.
Carnley, P. (2004). *Reflections in Glass.* Sydney: Harper Collins.
Carson, D.A. (1991) *The Gospel according to John* Leicester:IVP/Grand Rapids:
     Eerdmans
Dunzl, F. (. (2007). *A Brief History of the Doctrine of the Trinity in the Early
     Church.* London/New York: T & T Clark.
Foucault, M. (1980) 'Truth and Power' pp 109-133 in Gordon, C (ed.)
     Power/Knowledge. New York: Pantheon
France, R.T. (1985) *Matthew* Leicester: IVP.
Giles, K. (2002) *The Trinity and Subordinationism: the Doctrine of God and the
     Contemporary Gender Debate* Downers Grove: Illinois.
-----,   (2006). 'Father and Son: Divided or Undivided in Power and
     Authority.' Evangelical Theological Society. Washington, D.C.

-----., (2009) *Jesus and the Father: Modern Evangelicals Reinvent the Doctrine of the Trinity* Grand Rapids: Zondervan

-----., (2012) *The Eternal Generation of the Son: Maintaining Orthodoxy in Trinitarian Theology* Nottingham: IVP

Grillmeier, A. (1975). *Christ in Christian Tradition* (Vol 1) 2 rev. ed.. Trans. Bowden, J. London/Oxford: Mowbrays.

Gunton, C. (1993). *The One, the Three and the Many*. Cambridge: Cambridge University Press.

Hanson, R. (1988). *The Search for the Christian Doctrine of God: the Arian Controversy 318-381*. Edinburgh: T & T Clark.

Harvey, A.E. (1976). *Jesus on Trial - A study in the Fourth Gospel*. London: SPCK.

Holmes, S. 2015 'Reflections on a new defence of "complementarianism"' http://steverholmes.org.uk/blog/?p=7507 (accessed 08.04.2016)

Jeremias, J. (2012) The *Prayers of Jesus*. London: SCM.

Kant, I. (1784) 'What is Enlightenment?' http://www.allmendeberlin.de/What-is-Enlightenment.pdf (accessed 03.05.2015)

Köstenberger, A.J. (2004) *John* Grand Rapids: Baker.

La Cugna, C.M. (1991). *God for Us: The Trinity and Christian Life*. New York: Harper Collins.

Lampe, G.W.H. (1997). 'Christian Theology in the Patristic Period' in Cunliffe-Jones, H. (ed.) *A History of Christian Doctrine* Edinburgh: T & T Clark, pp. 21-180.

Lasch, C. (1978) *The Culture of Narcissism* New York: W. Norton

Lewis, C.S. (2001) *The Last Battle* London: HarperCollins (1st published 1956)

Lincoln, A.T. (2005) *The Gospel according to John*. Black's New Testament Commentaries. Continuum:London

Michaels, J Ramsey (2010) *The Gospel of John* Grand Rapids/Cambridge: Eerdmans

Mill, J.S. (2006) *On Liberty* Harmondsworth: Penguin (1st published 1859)

Moignt, J. (1970) 'Le Probleme du Dieu Unique chez Tertullien', *RSR* 44:337-362.

Moltmann, J. (1981). *The Trinity and the Kingdom of God: the doctrine of God* trans. Kohl, M. London SCM.

-----., (1991). *History and the Triune God*. Bowden, J. (Trans.) London: SCM.

Morris, L., (1995). Rev. ed. *The Gospel according to John*. NICNT. Grand Rapids: Eerdmans

Mounce, R.H. (1991) Matthew Peabody: Hendrickson/Carlisle: Paternoster

Nietzsche, F. (1882, 1887) *The Gay Science*

-----., (1883-5) *Thus Spake Zarathustra*

-----., (1886) *Beyond Good and Evil*

Neyrey, J. (1988). *An Ideology of Revolt*. Philadelphia: Fortress Press.

Osborn, E., (1997). *Tertullian, First Theologian of the West*. Cambridge: CUP.

Ovey, M.J., (2008) 'A Private Love? Karl Barth and the Triune God' pp 198-231 in *Engaging with Barth: Contemporary Evangelical Critiques* Nottingham: Apollos.

------., (2014) 'True Sonship – Where Dignity and Submission Meet' chapter 6 in *One God in Three Persons* (eds. Starke, J and Ware, B.A.) Wheaton: Crossway.

E. Petersen (1935) *Der Monotheismus als politisches Problem. Ein Beitrag zur Geschichte der politischen Theologie im Imperium Romanum.* Hegner, Leipzig ET in (2011) Theological Tractates (trans M.J. Hollerich) Stanford: Stanford University Press.

Pinnock, C (1989) 'Introduction' in Pinnock, C (ed.), *The Grace of God, the Will of Man.* Grand Rapids: Zondervan.

Rahner, K. (1970). *The Trinity.* Donceel, J. trans. London/New York: Burns and Oates.

Ridderbos, H., (1997) *The Gospel of John* Grand Rapids: Eerdmans

Schwartz, R.M. (1998) *The Curse of Cain: the Violent Legacy of Monotheism* Chicago: University of Chicago Press.

Smulders, P. (1944) *La Doctrine trinitaire de S. Hilaire de Poitiers* Rome: Universitatis Gregorianae.

Strauss, L. (2000) *On Tyranny* eds. Gourevitch, V. and Roth. M. Chicago: University of Chicago Press.

Talmon, J.L., (1986) *The Origins of Totalitarian Democracy* London: Penguin.

Thompson, M.M. (2000) *The Promise of the Father: Jesus and God in the New Testament.* Louisville: Westminster John Knox Press.

De Tocqueville, A. (1968) *Democracy in America* New York: Fontana. (2 vols) Trans Lawrence G. (1st published 1835)

Twenge, J. M. (2007) *Generation Me* New York: Free Press.

Twenge, J.M. and Campbell, W.K. (2009) *The Narcissism Epidemic: Living in the Age of Entitlement* New York: Free Press

Ulrich, J. (1994). *Die Anfänge de abendländischen Rezeption des Nizänums.* Berlin and New York: PTS.

Wells, S. (2009) 'Can we still call God Father?' Romans 8.12-17 A Sermon preached in Duke University Chapel on June 7, 2009 http://chapel-archives.oit.duke.edu/documents/sermons/June7CanwestillcallGodFather.pdf (accessed 13.11.2012)

Widdicombe, P. (2000). *The Fatherhood of God from Origen to Athanasius.* Oxford: OUP.

Wiles, M. (1996). *Archetypal Heresy: Arianism through the centuries.* Oxford: Clarendon.

Williams, R. (1979) 'Barth on the Triune God' pp 147-193 in Sykes, S W (ed.) *Karl Barth – Studies of his Theological Methods.* Oxford: Clarendon Press.

------. (1987). *Arius, Heresy and Tradition.* London: Dartman, Longman and Todd.

Witherington, B. (1995). *John's Wisdom - a Commentary on the Fourth Gospel.* Westminster: John Knox Press.

9.3   Index

If you have enjoyed this book, you might like to consider

- *supporting the work of the Latimer Trust*

- *reading more of our publications*

- *recommending them to others*

See www.latimertrust.org for more information.

LATIMER PUBLICATIONS

LATIMER PUBLICATIONS

LATIMER PUBLICATIONS

LATIMER PUBLICATIONS

Lightning Source UK Ltd.
Milton Keynes UK
UKOW01f1407160616

276363UK00002B/76/P